A BRIEF HISTORY *of*

EASTVALE

LOREN P. MEISSNER &
KIM JARRELL JOHNSON

Charleston London
THE History PRESS

Published by The History Press
Charleston, SC 29403
www.historypress.net

Front cover, upper: The San Gabriel Mountain range dominates the landscape north of Eastvale on a clear 2005 morning after a rain. *Courtesy Randy Bekendam, Southern California Agricultural Land Foundation.*

Front cover, lower: First-grade students at Eastvale in the fall of 1933 included Loren Meissner's sister Doris and Premier Ranch resident Victor Scamara Jr. *Courtesy Doris Meissner Klock.*

Back cover, inset: Eastvale School District served eight elementary grades from 1893 until 1947. The site of this one-room schoolhouse, occupied 1896–1913, is now the southeast corner of Chandler and Harrison Avenues. *Courtesy Riverside Public Library, Local History Collection.*

Back cover, lower: This ranch on Cloverdale Road was a premier example of the bucolic ambience of Eastvale's agrarian paradise, which lasted until the end of the Harada era (1959–90). *Courtesy JoAnn Harada Gunter.*

First published 2013

Manufactured in the United States

ISBN 978.1.60949.950.1

Library of Congress CIP data applied for.

This book is dedicated to the people of Eastvale, California. May they never forget their past and may their future be bright!

To know nothing of what happened before you were born is to remain forever a child.

—Cicero (106–43 BC)

CONTENTS

Preface

THE NAME, "EASTVALE"

The city of Eastvale in Riverside County, California, was incorporated on 1 October 2010. The *city* name is spelled as a single word, but when the *elementary school district* was created in 1893, its name was spelled with two words, as East Vale. The older spelling fell into disuse long before 1947 when

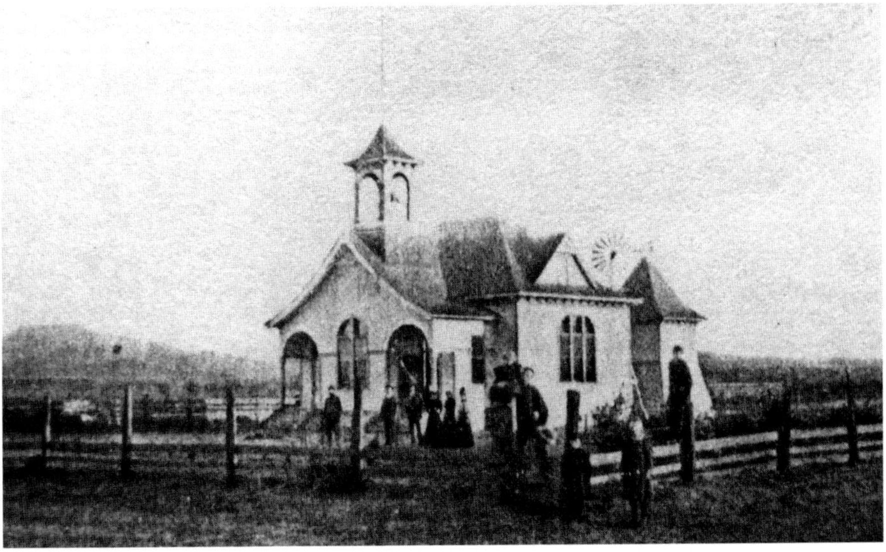

A one-room Eastvale schoolhouse at the southeast corner of present-day Chandler Street and Harrison Avenue, constructed soon after the district was created, was in use from fall 1896 until spring 1913. *Courtesy Riverside Public Library, Local History Collection.*

the elementary school was absorbed into Corona Unified School District (now Corona-Norco).

The earliest known reference to East Vale or Eastvale as a place name in California is found on a list of elementary school districts formed in 1893 along with Riverside County. The name was probably proposed by members of the Fuller family, who had recently established Pioneer Ranch next to the Santa Ana River, occupying several thousand acres of land in the new school district. A Fuller family member was on the first school board, and other families associated with the ranch supplied a significant portion of the student body.

History of the area before 1900 provides a few suggestions for the name origin. Family patriarch Harrison Fuller was born about seventy-five miles from Eastvale, Pennsylvania. There was a Valley School, where some of the pupils had been attending prior to 1893, less than two miles west of Fuller ranch headquarters; and the new school district may have been considered "the *East* campus of *Valley* elementary school." Milton Vale had a ranch near Archibald and Limonite (see Appendix A), and most territory in the new school district was *East* of the *Vale* ranch.

ACKNOWLEDGEMENTS

Many thanks to the people who shared their time so generously with us in the research for this book: Ike and Squeaker Bootsma, JoAnn Harada Gunter, Lynne Eldridge Richie, Susan Scamara, Victor Scamara Jr., Michelle Nissen, Bill Wilkman, Jim Hofer and Kevin Bash.

INTRODUCTION

The Santa Ana River arises at springs near the nine-thousand-foot level, on the north slope of San Gorgonio Mountain about twenty-five miles east of San Bernardino in Southern California. The river flows across the Inland Empire and through Santa Ana Canyon before its one-hundred-mile journey to the Pacific Ocean ends southeast of Los Angeles. About halfway along its route, the river passes Eastvale and defines the city's southern boundary.

Incorporated on 1 October 2010, Eastvale is still a new city, full of new houses, occupied by new residents. The population count grew from about 1,600 at the 1990 census to 6,000 in 2000 and more than 50,000 in 2010. Most of the 48,400 (or more) residents who arrived at Eastvale during the past twenty years have little inkling of the city's previous history. They may have learned from early residents that there were more dairy cows than people at Eastvale in 1990.

A Wide View

Imagine that you are sitting in a darkened theater, waiting to learn about the history of Eastvale. The curtain is still closed, but some barely audible activity is going on backstage—perhaps alluding to events as long ago as the conquest of the Aztec empire by Cortés in 1521. Although the details are not yet clear, you feel that the backstage stir has some significance that will soon be revealed.

The curtain rises, and the scene comes into focus at a location near present-day Eastvale, between 1821 and 1848. Alta California is a province of Mexico, newly independent from Spain. In the background, herds of cattle roam the mesa, along its shallow valleys and over its low hills, on ranchos that have been granted to prominent Mexican citizens.

Your peripheral vision is not limited by the narrow theater stage. The geographical sphere you are watching is Cinerama-wide, and you become aware of influences on Eastvale history from far beyond present-day city boundaries. For example, you learn that territory administered by Mission San Gabriel Arcángel (founded in 1771) was gradually extended eastward beyond San Bernardino, encompassing present-day Eastvale. And you hear about Arcadia Bandini, who lived for perhaps a year (1840) during her early teens at the large adobe residence on Rancho El Rincón near Eastvale and later (1880) became famous for her philanthropy at Santa Monica.

GEOGRAPHICAL SPHERE OF EASTVALE HISTORY

Still, the most important events of Eastvale's history, as viewed on a present-day screen, occurred within Southern California's Inland Empire—the populated and industrialized portion of the Upper Santa Ana River Basin north and east of Prado Dam. Historical documents frequently describe this Upper Basin as "the mesa" or "the tableland" since it is relatively flat, although punctuated with shallow gullies and clusters of low hills.

Snowmelt flows into this basin from three mountain ranges along the San Andreas Fault line, each of which has peaks higher than ten thousand feet above sea level. From southeast to northwest, these are the San Jacinto, San Bernardino and San Gabriel ranges. Mitchell describes the topography of the Upper Basin and the mountains that bound it:

> *The San Jacinto Mountains rise to 10,834 feet at San Jacinto Peak, and constitute the final eastern wall, preventing the coast and its cooling influences from reaching the desert. These mountains drain westward into the San Jacinto River, which feeds Lake Elsinore, which then drains into Temescal Wash, which joins the Santa Ana River in the Prado Basin.*

> *The San Bernardino Mountains, including 11,502-foot San Gorgonio Mountain, are the highest mountains in Southern California. The Santa Ana River proper begins just north of San Gorgonio Mountain. Fed by snowmelt and springs, the river here is more like a stream, 10 feet wide and fast moving.*
>
> *The San Gabriel Mountains rise to the west of, but in line with, the San Bernardino Mountains. Separated by the San Andreas Fault at the Cajon Pass, these mountains provide the snowy backdrop most Southern Californians enjoy on clear winter days* [as shown in the cover photo]. *Mt. Baldy, officially Mount San Antonio, sits atop the crest of this range at an elevation of 10,080 feet above sea level.*

The San Gabriel range drains southward. The Santa Ana River's two most westerly tributaries, San Antonio Creek and Cucamonga Creek, flow into Chino Creek, a stub that runs eastward from the Chino Hills and meets the river just above Prado Dam, a few miles west of Eastvale. Due principally to diversion of water for irrigation since 1900, San Antonio and Cucamonga Creeks are now seasonally dry in their lower reaches but can overflow during heavy rainfall. Cucamonga Creek is channeled through a corner of present-day Eastvale west of Archibald Avenue, entering the city near Limonite Avenue and exiting across Hellman Avenue just north of Chandler Street.

Mitchell's description continues:

> *The Chino Creek basin is a low-lying valley surrounded by mountains and hills, which form a bottleneck where the Santa Ana River squeezes between the Chino Hills and Santa Ana Mountains. Prado Dam was constructed at this bottleneck in 1941 to protect downstream areas from flooding. The wetlands and riparian forests behind the dam are today some of the most important habitats in Southern California, with more than 4000 acres of willow-cottonwood forest and other riparian and wetland communities.*

To a child growing up in Eastvale before the western horizon became cluttered with silhouettes of houses, the Chino Hills were "where the sun went" each evening. Their maximum elevation is less than two thousand feet.

The Santa Ana Mountains form the southern boundary of the Upper Santa Ana River Basin. Their highest summit, 5,700-foot Santiago Peak, is clearly visible south of Eastvale, behind Corona. This range, which continues southeastward past Temescal Canyon and Lake Elsinore, provides some shelter from coastal weather effects but obviously has less influence than the ranges of much higher mountains to the north and east.

TIME BOUNDARIES FOR EASTVALE HISTORY

Historical time boundaries are similarly broad. Anthropologists estimate that ancestors of California's aborigines crossed Bering Strait on a land bridge more than twenty thousand years ago and that primitive cultures in present-day Southern California had stabilized long before the era of recorded history began in China, Egypt or Babylon.

But prehistoric events within Eastvale's present-day 13.1-square-mile boundaries seem not to have attracted much notice. Explorers during the 1500s discovered harbors at San Diego, Monterey and San Francisco, but they did not penetrate the inland valleys. De Anza's overland treks from Sonora in 1774 and 1776 crossed the Santa Ana River near present-day Riverside and skirted Eastvale on the north.

Then, in 1838, Don Juan Bandini received a grant of land along the north side of the Santa Ana River that included all but a few acres of present-day Eastvale. Among surviving records from that year is the earliest known formal documentation of an event at Eastvale—the official survey of Bandini's Jurupa grant boundaries. This survey is the event that begins our story.

"Once upon a time…"

Chapter 1

LAND GRANTS: JURUPA 1838, EL RINCÓN 1839

Juan Bandini was the first individual of European descent to own land in present-day Eastvale—or in any part of what is now northwestern Riverside County. The Mexican governor of California authorized a pair of land grants to Bandini in this area: Jurupa grant in 1838 and El Rincón grant in 1839. Together, these stretched along the north side of the Santa Ana River for almost twenty miles, encompassing most of the land in the present-day cities of Eastvale and Jurupa Valley. These grants continued from Prado, just west of Corona, northeastward all the way to Colton.

Two individuals besides Juan Bandini played major roles in the history of Eastvale during the land grant era. Abel Stearns, a Massachusetts Yankee, strongly influenced the history of Southern California ranching and merchandising. He acquired Mexican citizenship in 1828 at age thirty, married Bandini's daughter Arcadia in 1841 and became owner of 85 percent of Jurupa land grant in 1859. Chapter 2 describes Don Abel's further role in early stages of the transition from cattle ranching to American-style diversified farming.

Leonardo Cota married Ynez Yorba and became patriarch of a family that, for more than sixty years, maintained the large adobe house constructed for Juan Bandini on El Rincón, in the southwest corner of present-day Riverside County, a little more than a mile west of the boundary of present-day Eastvale. This Bandini-Cota Adobe, at the brow of a mesa, was finally merged into Prado Flood Control Basin, and the structure disintegrated after maintenance was discontinued, but satellite maps still reveal an outline of the ruins.

1.1 Don Juan Lorenzo Bruno Bandini

First Individual Eastvale Landowner

An unusual incident took place on the bluff north of the Santa Ana River about 175 years ago, on 4 December 1838.

Don Juan Bandini became the first individual landowner in present-day Eastvale on 28 September 1838 when Juan Alvarado, governor of the Mexican province of Alta California, awarded him Jurupa land grant. The grant stretched along the north side of the Santa Ana River for about seventeen miles, between present-day Eastvale and Colton, and averaged about four miles in width. A survey was undertaken about two months later, in early December, to confirm the boundaries of Jurupa grant.

While three distinguished-looking *caballeros* (horsemen) watched, two *vaqueros* (cowboys) rode along the riverbank to conduct the survey. The two gentlemen witnessing the survey with Bandini were Luis Arenas, mayor of Los Angeles, and Don Carlos Dominguez, who represented the Yorba family, grantee of adjacent lands. Garner explains: "The measuring of the land was done on horseback. One rider would take one end of a lariat one hundred varas in length (slightly less than one hundred yards), and another rider would take the other end. The first man drove a number of long stakes tipped with iron into the ground every hundred varas. The second man pulled the stakes, by counting which they could tell how many varas had been measured off."

Boundaries

Riverside County historian W.D. Puntney quotes the 1838 survey record. Bandini's Jurupa grant began at a prominent hill that eventually came to be included within the city of Riverside and "ran for thirty thousand *varas* along the Santa Ana River to 'the point of the same tableland where Mr. Bandini had established the house and where the river makes a turn.' The property line then ran north, 'crossing between two springs of Guapan (probably Guapas)' for another seven thousand *varas* where 'the first sand hill' marked the northwest corner."

The "springs of Guapa" (spelled variously) near the southwest corner of Jurupa grant have long since ceased to flow, presumably because irrigation has lowered the water table. (See Appendix A.) They are shown as *ciénegas* (springs) on an 1888 irrigation map, near the northeast corner of present-day Hellman and Chandler Streets. The springs fed a basin called Mill Creek or Rincon Creek, which still collects seasonal runoff from Cucamonga Creek east of Hellman Avenue.

A dam, mill and mill ditch (hence the name Mill Creek) are shown on the 1888 map about a mile downstream from the *ciénegas*. An 1890 Rincon Tract description notes: "In one place a spring supplies some 250 inches of water, which is used to run the Chino valley grist-mill, being afterward turned to purposes of irrigation. This stream remains the same summer and winter, 'the lay of the land' being such that the rains affect it very little, while the summer droughts do not diminish the water supply." The mill was the Old Grist Mill, near Hellman and Chandler Streets, also shown on a map in Corona Library historical archives, annotated after 1971 by Christina Fear Desborough, who lived for a time in the nearby Cota family residence at El Rincón.

In 1974, anthropologists identified an old Gabrieleño village site called Guapa near this part of Cucamonga Creek, according to accounts by Gunther and by Langenwalter. Sites of other landmarks along the west and north sides of Jurupa grant can be approximated from surveys, which in 1879 confirmed the title to about forty-one thousand acres (sixty-four square miles) of land.

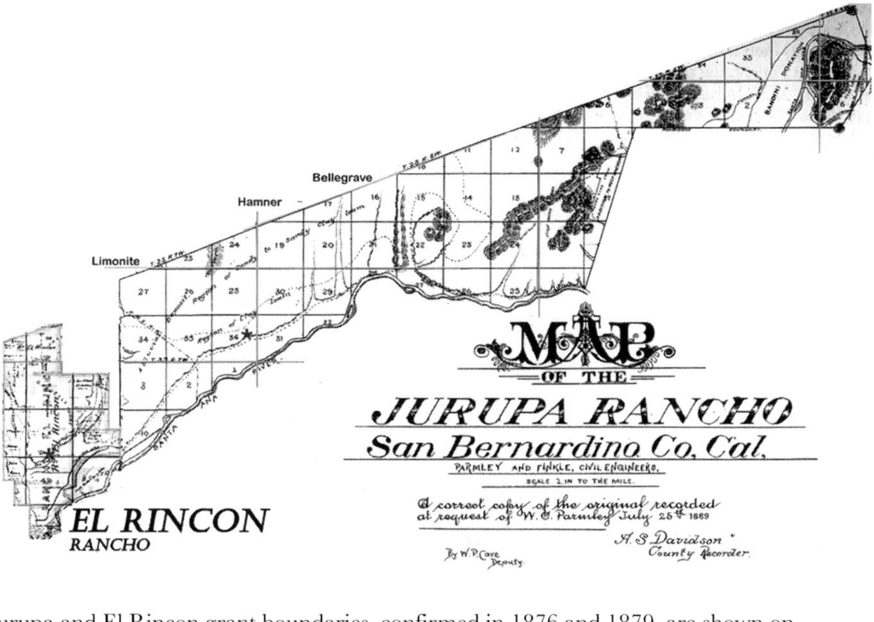

Jurupa and El Rincon grant boundaries, confirmed in 1876 and 1879, are shown on this 1888 map. A railroad from Pomona through present-day Eastvale had recently been surveyed and graded but was never completed. Present-day names added by Loren Meissner. *Courtesy David Rumsey Historical Map Collection.*

The western boundary of the surveyed grant now forms a segment of the Riverside–San Bernardino County line along Hellman Avenue and is a part of Eastvale's city limit on the west. The site of the sand hill mentioned in the 1838 survey report is near the point where Hellman Avenue turns eastward to connect with Limonite Avenue, at the northwest corner of present-day central Eastvale. The grant line then continues toward the northeast, along the alignment of Remington and Bellegrave Avenues, for about seventeen miles, intersecting the Santa Ana River again near Colton. The entire Jurupa grant was within present-day Riverside County, except for a small area at the northeast corner near Colton.

The Secularization Act

The land grant era began after Mexico gained independence from Spain in 1821. During the first twelve years of independence, Mexico was unable to settle on a suitable role for California's major institutions: the missions, the *presidios* (military establishments) and the *pueblos* (towns for inhabitants not directly connected with the missions), which dated from Spain's colonization of California a half century earlier. The most controversial question was what to do with mission lands, which had originally been the domain of native Californians. Almost all the land in coastal valleys, from San Diego north past San Francisco to Sonoma, had been incorporated into ranchos controlled by the Spanish-era missions. Present-day northwestern Riverside County, including Eastvale, was within the jurisdiction of Mission San Gabriel Arcángel. (See Appendix A.)

Finally, in August 1833, the Mexican government passed the Secularization Act. Riverside County historian Steve Lech describes the results of this process:

> *Instead of relinquishing the mission holdings to the Indians, this Act effectively closed the missions and remanded their vast tracts of land over to the California governor for dispersal as he saw fit. The missions were "secularized," and each was placed in charge of an administrator outside the jurisdiction of the Church. Beginning with the Secularization Act's implementation in 1834, and continuing until the end of Mexican rule in 1846, several successive governors divided former mission lands into approximately seven hundred Mexican land grants, called ranchos, which were given to friends, relatives, political cronies, wealthy citizens, and others who wished to have a piece of California.*

From among the qualifications for grants on this list, Juan Bandini would be described most appropriately as a "political crony."

Don Juan Lorenzo Bruno Bandini was born in Lima, Peru, in 1800 and migrated to San Diego at about the time of Mexican independence. His loyalty to local interests found favor with most of the thirteen "revolving-door" governors who served Mexican California during as many years between 1822 and 1836. In 1833, California's ruling council (*diputación*) elected Bandini to the Congress at Mexico City, where he promoted what he perceived to be the best interests of California.

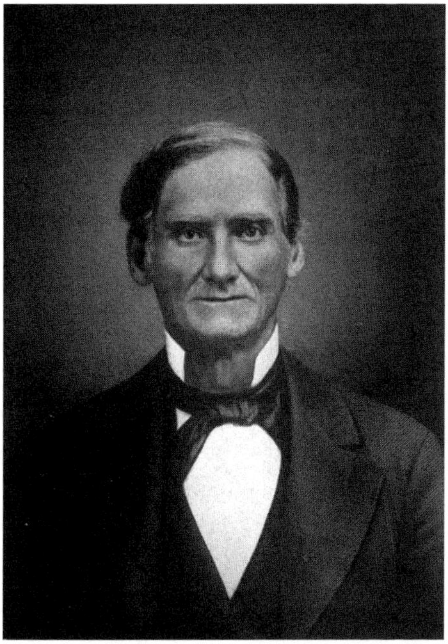

Juan Bandini. *Courtesy Wikimedia Commons.*

In 1838, Governor Alvarado appointed Juan Bandini as lay administrator of the secularized mission at San Gabriel. Later in the same year, on 28 September, Alvarado approved Bandini's petition for a grant of land in the Santa Ana River Valley.

Guapa Trail Junction

The river valley was already well known to travelers. In particular, the springs of Guapa near the western boundary of present-day Eastvale were a landmark on trails through the area, welcomed as a haven for rest and rejuvenation.

Travelers from Sonora in northern Mexico passed the springs on their way to San Gabriel and Los Angeles. The Sonora Trail from Yuma traversed Temescal Canyon and crossed the Santa Ana River near Guapa. Continuing upstream along Chino Creek to the vicinity of present-day Pomona, the trail then turned west and proceeded toward San Gabriel.

According to early histories of this route, the first Americans known to have traveled through Temescal Canyon were David Jackson's party of fur traders in 1831, on their return trip from San Gabriel to Santa Fe, New Mexico. Their eastbound route ran from San Gabriel through present-day Pomona, Chino, Rincon, Corona, Temescal Canyon, Lake Elsinore and Temecula.

This part of the Sonora Trail later became the Southern California portion of the Southern Emigrant Trail, connecting with Santa Fe during and after the gold rush. Many herds of cattle and sheep were driven along this road, which was later adopted as the Butterfield Overland Stage Route between 1858 and 1861. Pioneer wagons especially preferred this southern route during snowy weather, but they were plagued by the deserts between New Mexico and southeastern California.

Another trail branch was developed southwestward from Guapa through Santa Ana Canyon, connecting with coastal points including Mission San Juan Capistrano and the port of San Pedro.

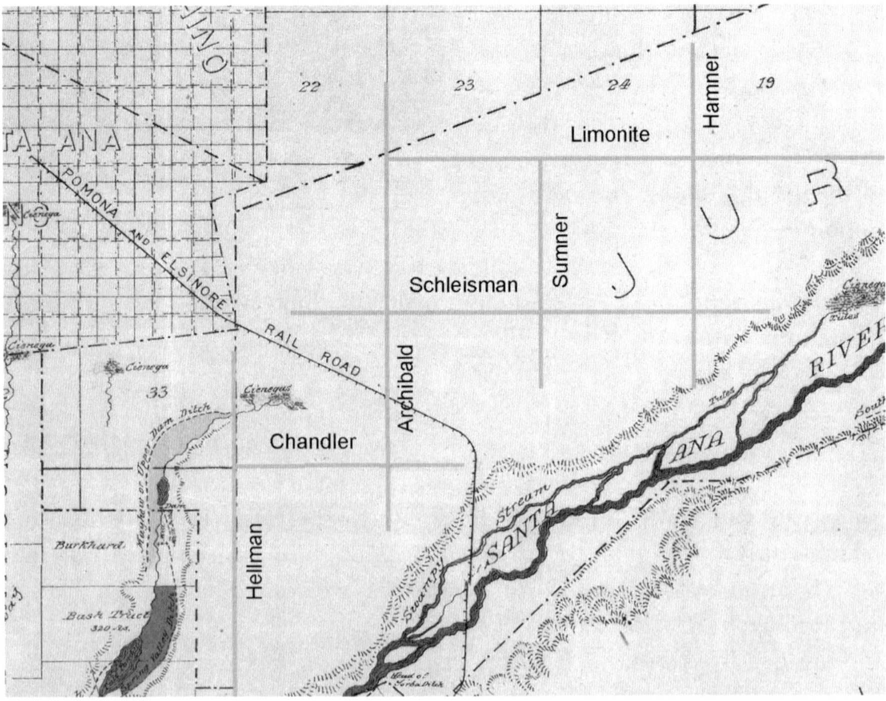

This detail from an 1888 irrigation survey map shows present-day central Eastvale (with main roads added for orientation) at the southwest corner of Jurupa land grant. The Pomona and Elsinore Railroad was graded but never completed. Between Chandler and Schleisman is the probable site of Guapa Springs, a popular resting place before 1800 on trails across the desert from Sonora to San Gabriel Mission. Present-day names added by Loren Meissner. *Courtesy David Rumsey Historical Map Collection.*

Between 1886 and 1889, hopes were high for a railroad line from Pomona to Elsinore, passing near Guapa and through present-day Eastvale, crossing the Santa Ana River a mile and a half west of Hamner Avenue. This railroad route, which appears prominently on the 1888 irrigation map, was mostly graded before July 1888, but the project was abandoned when anticipated support from Southern Pacific Railroad did not materialize.

"Road from Jurupa to Guapa"

An 1856 survey map records a trail variation through present-day Eastvale. Beginning in 1853, fifteen years after Bandini's survey of Jurupa grant boundaries, the U.S. General Land Office sent Henry Hancock to make formal surveys throughout the southern part of the new state of California. One of Hancock's maps records his 1856 survey of "Township 2 South,

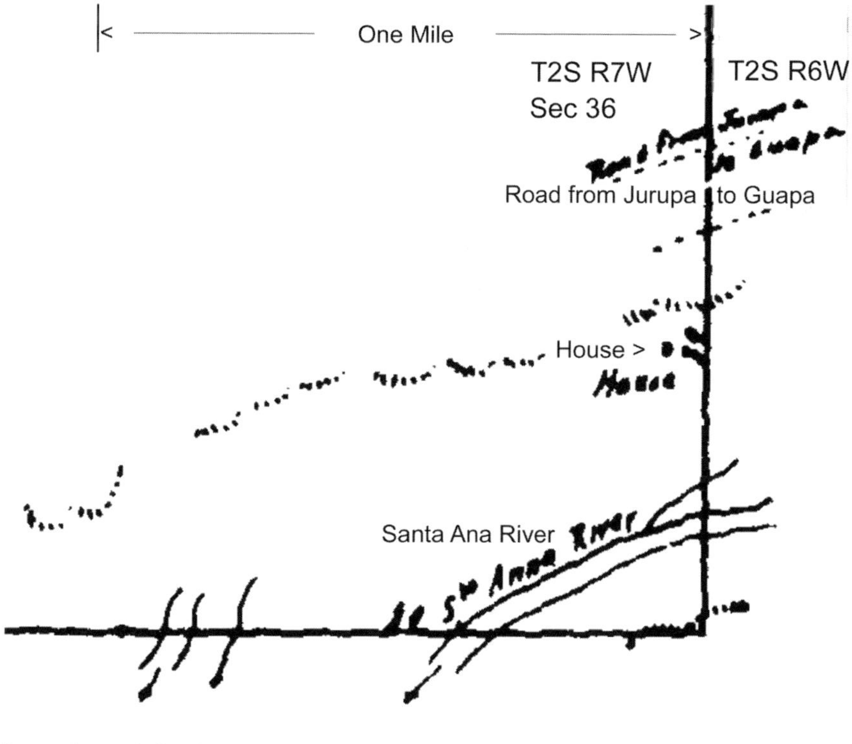

The north–south line is a survey boundary along the present-day Hamner Avenue alignment. *Map from Greenwood & Foster.*

Range 7 West," the southeast corner of which is located at the present-day Hamner Avenue bridge over the Santa Ana River, just west of the Interstate 15 crossing. The survey map notes a "Road from Jurupa to Guapa" and a "House" north of the river.

This road through Jurupa was popular even before Mexican independence. It was preferred for trips from San Gabriel Mission to its San Bernardino outpost as a way of avoiding the Cucamonga desert. Eastbound travelers followed the Sonora Trail from San Gabriel to present-day Pomona, turned south along Chino Creek to the Guapa junction and then branched northeastward along the Santa Ana River Valley or on the bluff at the north side to Jurupa and the mission outpost. (See Appendix A.)

A portion of this Jurupa-Guapa Road passed near such latter-day Eastvale landmarks as the site of the first Eastvale schoolhouse adjacent to Fuller Ranch headquarters at the corner of Harrison and Chandler Streets, Eleanor Roosevelt High School campus on Scholar Way (formerly Cleveland Avenue) and the Eastvale Fire Station on Hamner Avenue. A partially completed Santa Ana River regional trail now approximates this route.

Bandini Residence on Jurupa Grant

The group who surveyed the boundaries of Bandini's Jurupa grant on 4 December 1838 followed or paralleled the Jurupa-Guapa Road, bordering the Santa Ana River Valley along the north side.

One especially intriguing feature in the December 1838 report of the Jurupa grant survey is its mention of the "tableland where Mr. Bandini had established the house." Requirements for confirming a Mexican land grant included establishing a residence, and the adobe house on the mesa was constructed during the ten weeks that had elapsed since Governor Alvarado's grant to Juan Bandini on 28 September. (See Appendix A.)

Besides the reference in the 1838 survey, only one other contemporary reference to Bandini's residence on Jurupa grant is known. A Belgian named Augustin Janssens visited Juan Bandini on Jurupa grant before 1840. Janssens had been associated with Bandini in an 1834 project aimed at establishing Mexican colonies in Southern California, and he traveled throughout the region for several years afterward. Janssens reported, "The ranch was level, valuable, and prosperous. The San Bernardino [*sic*] river flowed through it...One could see across the plain all the way to Cucamonga."

Bandini Jurupa Adobe Site

The residence that Bandini "had established," as mentioned in the December 1838 survey report, is probably the "House" indicated on Hancock's 1856 U.S. survey map, just north of the Santa Ana River on the west side of present-day Hamner Avenue, within Eastvale city limits.

Correspondence between 1925 and 1931 among well-known Southern California historians George William Beattie, Janet Williams Gould and Frank Rolfe is preserved in the Gould collection at Corona Public Library.

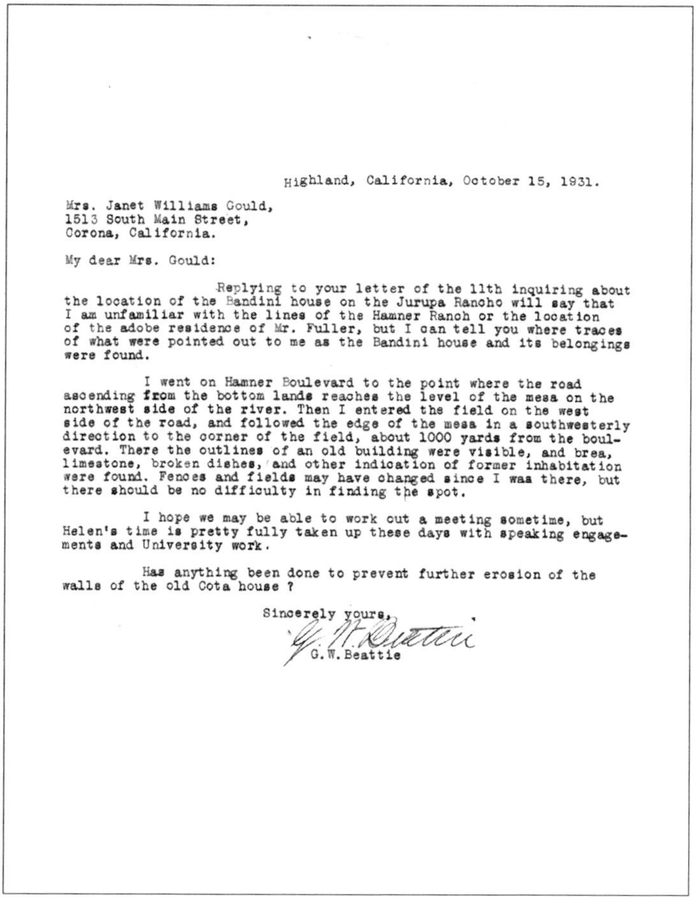

Highland, California, October 15, 1931.

Mrs. Janet Williams Gould,
1513 South Main Street,
Corona, California.

My dear Mrs. Gould:

Replying to your letter of the 11th inquiring about the location of the Bandini house on the Jurupa Rancho will say that I am unfamiliar with the lines of the Hamner Ranch or the location of the adobe residence of Mr. Fuller, but I can tell you where traces of what were pointed out to me as the Bandini house and its belongings were found.

I went on Hamner Boulevard to the point where the road ascending from the bottom lands reaches the level of the mesa on the northwest side of the river. Then I entered the field on the west side of the road, and followed the edge of the mesa in a southwesterly direction to the corner of the field, about 1000 yards from the boulevard. There the outlines of an old building were visible, and brea, limestone, broken dishes, and other indication of former inhabitation were found. Fences and fields may have changed since I was there, but there should be no difficulty in finding the spot.

I hope we may be able to work out a meeting sometime, but Helen's time is pretty fully taken up these days with speaking engagements and University work.

Has anything been done to prevent further erosion of the walls of the old Cota house ?

Sincerely yours,
G. W. Beattie
G.W. Beattie

Historian G.W. Beattie wrote a letter to Janet Gould in 1931 describing "traces of what were pointed out to me as the Bandini house" during an earlier visit to Eastvale. *Courtesy Corona Public Library, W.D. Addison Heritage Room.*

Beattie had visited the site of an old adobe building, possibly at the same location as the House on the 1856 map.

Rolfe wrote to Gould in 1927, calling attention to Beattie's 1925 journal article. Rolfe's letter also mentions that Beattie "has located the ruins of the old Jurupa ranch house which are not far north of Corona."

Responding to Gould's later inquiry, Beattie wrote in October 1931: "I can tell you where traces of what were pointed out to me as the Bandini house and its belongings were found. I went [north from Norco] on Hamner Boulevard to the point where the road ascending from the bottom lands reaches the level of the mesa on the northwest side of the river. Then I entered the field on the west side of the road, and followed the edge of the mesa in a southwesterly direction to the corner of the field, about 1000 yards from the boulevard. There the outlines of an old building were visible, and brea [tar or pitch], limestone, broken dishes, and other indication of former inhabitation were found."

The letter from Beattie does not mention the identity of whoever "pointed out" the site to him. Appendix A suggests that it was Walter T. Garner (1877–1949). There is reason to believe that Beattie's "1000 yards" is an overestimate, but sources describe traces of Bandini's 1838 residence, on the bluff north of the Santa Ana River west of Hamner, well into the twentieth century. The Pine, Ashcroft and Walkinshaw family members occupied the house temporarily for short periods until about 1880. When the roof was later taken off to be used in building another house, the adobe soon melted down. (See Appendix A.)

On 21 June 1933, the Women's Progressive Club of Norco placed a marker near Hamner Avenue on the bluff north of the river, close to the site of the present Eastvale fire station. The ceremony was proposed by Janet Gould on the basis of her correspondence with Beattie, as reported in Corona and Los Angeles newspapers. Unfortunately, the marker was vandalized and disappeared a few months later.

Jurupa—El Rincón Merger

For at least a year after acquiring Jurupa grant, Juan Bandini resided mainly at San Gabriel, where he was still administrator, while some family members occupied the Jurupa adobe residence.

But Bandini already had his eye on another nearby piece of property. Deciding he needed a more elegant dwelling where he could entertain guests, he had noticed some unclaimed farmland with an excellent view just west of the Guapa trail junction.

Six weeks after the Jurupa grant survey, on 21 January 1839, Juan Bandini submitted a successful petition to Governor Alvarado for 4,400 additional acres or about seven square miles, which came to be known as El Rincón grant (translated as *The Corner*), adjoining the west side of his Jurupa grant. A tiny segment of El Rincón is now within the city of Eastvale, extending south from where the county line turns west just south of River Road.

There are indications that construction of Bandini's second adobe house (later known as the Bandini-Cota Adobe), on El Rincón grant, was completed by the end of 1840. After Bandini moved to the new house, he treated Jurupa and El Rincón grants as a single ranch, which he called San Juan del Rio. Many of Bandini's letters and other historical records do not distinguish between Jurupa and El Rincón portions of the combined ranch when they describe specific later events (such as the death in April 1841 of Juan's father, José Bandini). But it seems clear that Don Juan no longer considered the earlier Jurupa adobe as his residence. During 1841 and 1842 there were five daughters and four sons in the Bandini family, all living at the adobe on El Rincón.

A study of the Prado Basin by Johnson and Buchel describes the Bandini-Cota adobe in detail:

> *Unlike the modest adobe located on Jurupa grant, the new house was unusual for its time, with two stories, huge rooms and floors made of wood hauled from the San Bernardino Mountains. Among the furnishings were a harp and a piano, the latter said to be the first ever shipped around Cape Horn. In addition to its silver, the family was particularly proud of the tall Florentine mirror and stand, and an ornate couch and chairs. Another treasure was the painting which Queen Isabel is said to have given to Columbus.*
>
> *Besides cattle, Bandini's records show that the combined ranch included a vineyard, as well as plots of beans and pumpkins and fields of wheat, corn and barley. The large resident labor force consisted mainly of native day laborers and house servants, who were paid according to a fairly typical relationship between patron and Indian laborer in the late Hispanic period. There were also vaqueros who tended the cattle, as well as overseers.*
>
> *During 1841 and 1842, Juan Bandini, wife, children (all under age 14), Juan's father, and servants were in permanent residence. Visitors, mostly relatives, passed through occasionally. Bandini was a true aristocrat,*

by California standards. However, he came to Rincon trying to bounce back from a financial disaster. He used his ranch to breed horses for sale to New Mexico, and cattle to dispose of in the hide and tallow market. Slaughtering was probably done on some distant portion of his vast estates. He grew various crops with seeming success. Bandini was also a timber merchant and mining speculator while at Rincon. However, it appears that none of his enterprises were lucrative.

Life was slow-paced, lonely, isolated, hot and dirty. The ranch had to be fairly self-sufficient. There were only enough funds for such non-local goods as sugar, imported cloth, medicine, and occasional treats like coffee and tea. A lot of people had to be accounted for, a lot of mouths fed, a lot of bodies clothed. Owning such a ranch was a tremendous responsibility; if a good life was to be had, it was through good management and some clever twisting of the urban merchants' arms. For the most part, the few pleasures of life were simple ones. For example, Arcadia Bandini remembered well the joy of swimming in the river.

Bandini Leaves Jurupa—El Rincón

Juan Bandini did not maintain an extended presence in the Jurupa–El Rincón area. In 1842, he moved to San Juan Capistrano, having been appointed administrator of the new village of Indians near the secularized mission site. He had already sold a portion of El Rincón to Bernardo Yorba in 1841, and he sold the remainder in 1843. Also in 1843, Bandini sold about 15 percent of the land area of his Jurupa grant, at the eastern end, most of which was later developed by Louis Robidoux and included the present-day downtown portion of the city of Riverside. Bandini maintained absentee ownership of the remaining 85 percent of Jurupa, including present-day Eastvale, which he kept as a large-scale cattle ranch until 1859 when he ceded it to his son-in-law, Abel Stearns.

1.2 Background: Mission San Gabriel Arcángel

Spanish Colonization in California

In the mid-1700s, the Spanish Crown recognized the need for a presence along the California coast to establish its claim against perceived threats of incursion by British, Russian or French colonists. The Franciscan religious order gladly agreed to establish missions, which were to be accompanied by *presidios* and *pueblos*.

The Franciscans planned to bring native Californians into the missions, where they would become "civilized" and Christianized. Their lands were to be held in trust and ultimately returned to the Europeanized converts. Similar plans had succeeded elsewhere in the Western Hemisphere, but the California natives did not respond as expected, mainly because the worldview of these primitive societies proved profoundly irreconcilable with that of the missionaries.

As one major example, this native hunter-gatherer society had no concept of landownership. Furthermore, the work schedule of the males had consisted of long periods of inactivity interspersed with short periods of strenuous labor whenever food became more easily available by hunting for animals or harvesting natural grains, berries and nuts. This contrasted sharply with the expectation of the Padres, who deplored "idleness" and demanded a more continuous, though perhaps less vigorous, level of effort.

Monroy notes that in the Indian worldview, certain spirits, which formed part of a being's essence, animated plants and animals—indeed everything in their small worlds necessary for their subsistence. They had to be assuaged correctly for humans to appropriate them. People produced when they were hungry, and the availability of food and the seasons determined when the work was done. When the Europeans came, they determined that these important attitudes regarding land, work and the animals had to change.

The missions exchanged tallow and hides from cattle raised on the ranchos for luxuries from foreign lands and necessities that could not be produced locally. There was no significant trade in beef, due primarily to lack of storage facilities. Meanwhile, cattle ranching and other farming activities on the ranchos literally rode roughshod over the fragile primitive plant and animal ecosystem that had supported the natives' hunter-gatherer lifestyle.

Mission San Gabriel Arcángel in 1827

Mission San Gabriel Arcángel was founded in 1771 by Father Junípero Serra, fourth in the chain of California missions after San Diego, Carmel and San Antonio de Padua. The Mission Fathers hoped not only to convert and civilize the natives in their immediate area but also to reach out into the territory surrounding each of the missions. The extent of lands administered from San Gabriel reached inland past San Bernardino and included present-day Eastvale.

Father José Sanchez, missionary of San Gabriel, reported on the outreach of the mission in 1827—six years after Mexico won independence from Spain in 1821. The territorial government asked for a report concerning the status of the mission, and Sanchez replied, "Toward the southeast, the [Mission] land extends through the cañon in the direction of the Colorado River for over twenty leagues. [A league is about three miles.] On this tract are the two sites La Puente, about four leagues, and Santa Ana, about ten leagues. At a distance of about fifteen leagues is another called Jorupet, while the distance to San Bernardino is about twenty leagues. In the same direction is the place called San Gorgonio, about twenty-seven leagues distant."

The three most distant sites on this list were established by the officials at Mission San Gabriel Arcángel—San Bernardino, Jurupa and San Gorgonio. The site called *Jorupet* in the Sanchez report, some fifteen leagues or forty-five miles east of the mission, obviously corresponds to Jurupa.

A translation of the 1827 Sanchez report appears in the book *San Gabriel Mission,* written one hundred years later, in 1927, by Zephyrin Engelhardt,

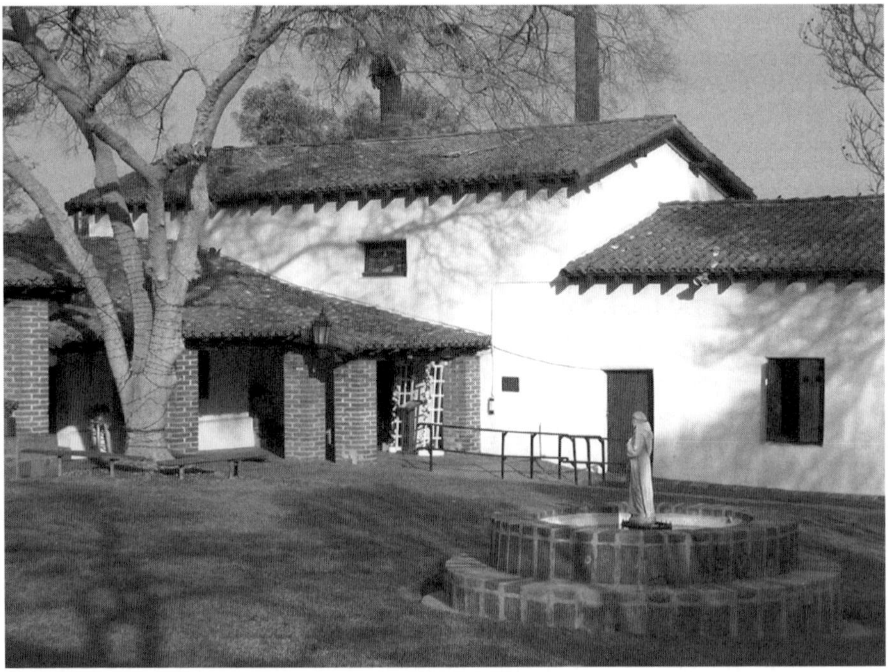

Restored San Gabriel Mission outpost at Redlands, originally established about 1819. *Courtesy San Bernardino County Museum Marketing Department.*

a historian at the restored Mission San Gabriel Arcángel. Engelhardt also quotes a local population statistic for the mission itself from Harrison Rogers, who visited San Gabriel in 1826 with Jedediah Smith's trapping expedition to California: "They have upwards of 1,000 persons employed, men, women, and children, Indians of different nations."

A mission *estancia* (outpost) on Rancho San Bernardino was established at Redlands in 1819 to supervise activities on San Gabriel's ranchos in the inland valleys and on tablelands south of Cajon Pass.

The outpost was located on Rancho San Bernardino, and the area under its administration soon encompassed the other two inland ranchos, Rancho San Gorgonio farther east and Rancho Jurupa to the southwest. These three ranchos must have accounted for at least half of San Gabriel's inventory. "The number of cattle which the Mission possesses, according to the reports it annually transmits to the government, will reach more or less 18,400 head; of horses, 2,400 in all; of mules, 130; of sheep, 14,000; of pigs, 150; of goats, 50; all very adapted to the country or lands, as experience has demonstrated."

1.3 JURUPA: ABEL STEARNS

A Yankee in Mexican California

The true champion of Eastvale and Jurupa Valley history during the Mexican era was not Juan Bandini, whose residence on the Santa Ana River Valley lands lasted less than three years. It was a Yankee named Abel Stearns, whose influence lasted until his death in 1871.

Stearns was a Yankee in Mexican California, according to D.M. Wright's biography. He was born in Massachusetts in 1798. His ancestors had come from England before 1700, and Abel was the third oldest of six sons and four daughters. His mother and father both died before he reached the age of fourteen. Some sources state or imply that Abel Stearns's ancestry was Jewish, but further search to date seems to contradict this. The story of Abel Stearns is in many ways a typical American success story. It is the history of a young New Englander who early had to make his own way and who chose, in true American fashion, to go west and seek his fortune. In order to earn his own living he went to sea, in good New England tradition.

His travels took Stearns to the Orient and then in 1826 to Mexico, where he became a naturalized citizen of Mexico's newly independent republic,

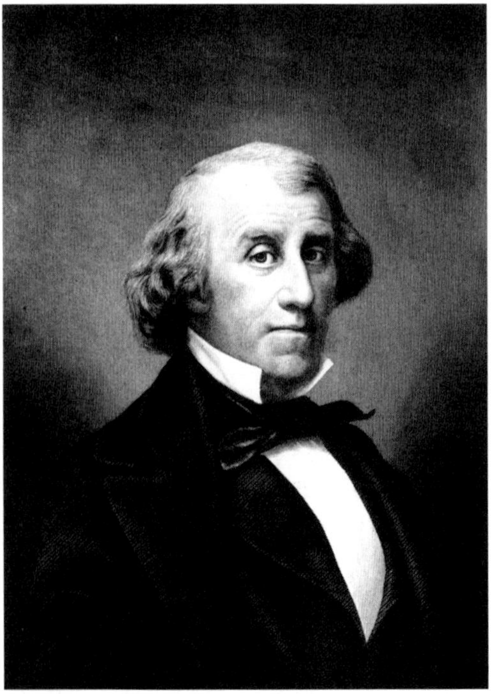

Abel Stearns, "Yankee in Mexican California," married Arcadia Bandini. *Courtesy USC Digital Library.*

hoping to improve his prospects. He finally settled in California, where his energetic Yankee approach to problems often gave him an edge over the instincts of the more easygoing Hispanic-trained Dons.

An early example was the trading post he established near Los Angeles in 1834. Previously, merchants arriving by sea had to tour the Los Angeles area ranchos, looking for hides and tallow ready to be exported in exchange for their imported goods. Stearns established a warehouse and centralized trading point on the nearby coast at San Pedro. Hides and tallow were now ready at the beach whenever ships arrived, and rancheros could acquire imported merchandise without a long wait for the next ship. It was Abel Stearns who took the first decisive step toward providing Los Angeles with a seaport. It took the energy and business acumen of a Yankee to recognize that the whole vast agricultural region of the Los Angeles area could be organized and exploited profitably, in an economic sense, by providing for the rancheros an easy way of marketing their products.

Stearns and Bandini

Juan Bandini met Abel Stearns in San Diego in 1829. Two years later, when Manuel Victoria was governor of Mexican California, Stearns offended Victoria and was deported on a ship. But a storm off the coast forced the ship to land at San Diego. There Stearns united with Bandini, who had been planning a revolt against Victoria. Stearns and Bandini continued as friends and political allies.

In May 1841, Abel Stearns married Juan Bandini's fourteen-year-old daughter, Arcadia. After 1848 during the early part of the American era, Stearns helped Juan Bandini maintain his vast tracts of land, which stretched from Tijuana to the San Bernardino Mountains. According to P. Baker:

> *Seeking relief from boredom, Juan turned his boundless energy to numerous wild business schemes. In 1850 Juan invested $15,000 to build the Gila House* [at San Diego], *an inn and general store, to accommodate the gold seekers traveling from Mexico to Sacramento. In December, Juan borrowed $10,000 from a French gambler at four percent monthly interest. When Bandini could not meet the payments, the Frenchman gave him an extension, but required the mortgage on both Bandini's home and store. In 1851 Bandini was surprised to discover that "all of a sudden trade left entirely."*
>
> *In order to pay his debts, Juan hurried down to* [his] *Rancho Guadalupe, near Tijuana, to market the goods from the Rancho. But to Bandini's amazement the Rancho had gone to seed and he hired a new supervisor and workers.*
>
> *While Bandini was at the Rancho his son-in-law, Charles Johnson* [husband of Dolores Bandini], *took the occasion to describe the entire family crisis to Abel Stearns: Don Juan's costly business schemes, the gambling proclivities of the don's young sons, and the expenditures of Doña Refugia Bandini in preparing one elegant fiesta after another even while feeling "awfully downcast" about money matters. Johnson estimated that a loan of $2,000 and proper management could save the Bandini estate and even make it profit "handsomely." Stearns took over the mortgage and saved Bandini from bankruptcy.*
>
> *However, when Juan ignored the repeated pleas of his son-in-law for sanity and realism in his business endeavors, the Bandini sons-in-law withdrew all financial help. They remained friendly towards Juan, but they carried on family matters without his advice. This caused Juan to complain of having lost respect. He no longer found himself the revolutionary of former days; instead, he was merely the father of numerous children who had to bail him out of his financial troubles, which were caused not only by his business failures, but also because he was a pace-setter in the social circles. He was one of the early California socialites and his wife often threw elegant fiestas which cost Juan as much as $1,000.*

Meanwhile, as Cleland points out, Stearns had begun his new career as a landowner and *ranchero*—a career that in time made him almost a legendary figure in the history of California. His long residence in the country and intimate knowledge of the business affairs and financial difficulties of all the large landholders enabled him to add one ranch after another to his holdings on highly advantageous terms.

Partly as payment for accumulated debts, in 1856 Bandini mortgaged to Stearns the 85 percent of his Jurupa grant that he still owned. The mortgage was settled three years later by a deed conveying Bandini's remaining interest in Rancho Jurupa to Stearns. The deed was dated 19 August 1859. Bandini died on 4 November 1859, less than three months later (see also Chapter 2). By 1860, Abel Stearns was the most important landowner in Southern California and owned all or major portions of Rancho La Habra, Rancho Los Coyotes, Rancho San Juan Cajón de Santa Ana, Rancho Las Bolsas, Rancho La Bolsa Chica, Rancho Jurupa and Rancho La Sierra.

Arcadia Stearns Baker née Bandini

Arcadia, Juan Bandini's oldest child, was born in San Diego on 12 January 1827. Of her childhood nothing is known, except that the Bandini home was always a center of social and political affairs. The girl early lost her mother, and when she was about eight years old her father remarried. (See Appendix A.) Arcadia's recollections include living at the Bandini residence on El Rincón grant at age thirteen or fourteen, where she enjoyed swimming in the Santa Ana River.

On 22 June 1841, at age fourteen, Arcadia married Abel Stearns at Mission San Gabriel Arcángel. They lived in a handsome house in the Pueblo of Los Angeles, at what is now the corner of Main and Arcadia Streets, known because of its size as the Palace: *El Palacio de Don Abel*.

Abel and Arcadia had no children. Arcadia's principal role in life was to act as hostess for frequent social events at *El Palacio*. As Abel Hoffman notes, Arcadia wrote of the care that had to be taken lest her dress be dirtied by the mud in the street and of the fact that the women put a lot of green, red and white into their ball gowns as a subtle message to the Americans about the loyalty of Californio women. Don Abel was not always present—he spent much of his time on business interests—but Arcadia earned a reputation for being friendly and generous to guests and family alike.

Arcadia was forty-four years old in August 1871 when Abel Stearns died. As described in Chapter 2, fortunes were on the rise in Southern California during Arcadia's years as a landholder. The weather problems of the 1860s had eased, and titles to most land grants had recently been certified—or soon would be. The rancho lands that Stearns had accumulated were now extremely valuable assets, ready to be subdivided and converted into small farms and villages.

It is said that Arcadia was strong when it came to business but was also compassionate and kind to those in need. A major project over the next several decades was fulfillment of Arcadia's vision for development of the city of Santa Monica and surrounding beach and parkland. She enlisted the cooperation of two neighboring landowners: Colonel Robert Symington Baker (1826–1894), who became her second husband in April 1875, and Nevada senator John Perceval Jones. They donated land for churches, schools, parks and a veterans' hospital. After Baker died in 1894, Arcadia took a third husband, John Gaffey.

When Arcadia died in 1912, she left a fortune estimated at between $7 and $8 million, at that time the largest probated estate in Los Angeles history.

In 1987, the City of Santa Monica dedicated a monument to Arcadia in memory of her love and devotion to Santa Monica and generous contributions of land to benefit the people and for the development of the city.

1.4 EL RINCÓN: LEONARDO COTA

A Wedding Present for Ynez Yorba

In November 1847, Leonardo Cota (1816–1877) married Ynez (1827–1911), a daughter of Don Bernardo Yorba, who owned El Rincón at that time. As a wedding gift, Don Bernardo gave his daughter the Bandini adobe with a portion of surrounding land. Most of El Rincón remained Yorba family property.

He had already given Ynez an adobe on the Rancho Cañon de Santa Ana, so Bernardo Yorba's deeding of the adobe on El Rincón to her in 1850 was an extraordinary gift. In the deed, prepared in his hand, Bernardo praised Ynez's service, obedience and daughterly love and stated that this gift was independent of whatever inheritance she might receive. He wrote that the other children were to respect his wishes and refrain from any attempt to touch this parcel. Indicative of the unstable period in which he was writing (see Chapter 2), he further stated that should there arise problems in the ownership of this home and piece of land, she would be entitled to another of equal quality.

A few acres of El Rincón grant land are included within Eastvale city limits, at the southwest corner. But this small piece of land does not include the Bandini-Cota Adobe site, which is about a mile farther west. Perhaps the southern half of El Rincón, which is within Riverside County, would have been more seriously considered for inclusion within Eastvale city boundaries if it were not part of the Prado Flood Basin.

Leonardo

When he married Ynez Yorba, Leonardo Cota was already a respected figure in the Southland. He had achieved success as a Mexican officer during the Battle of San Pasqual near San Diego in December 1846. In local politics, his speaking skills produced results, including adoption of a local ordinance he proposed requiring equal treatment of Indians before the law.

After about 1840, during the last years prior to the death of his father, Guillermo Cota (1768–1844), Leonardo assumed the position of family leader. He put Cota family affairs in order after his father's death. The family no longer owned any land except for the family residence, but before his marriage, Leonardo successfully petitioned for several grants of vacant land in and near Los Angeles Pueblo.

Beyond his immediate family circle, he assisted members of his mother's Nieto family and of his wife's Yorba family with legal matters. The man who would come to manage El Rincón as part of Bernardo Yorba's larger operation had, at an early age, established himself as a regional and family leader.

The Cota Family

The Cota family occupied the historic Bandini-Cota Adobe on El Rincón for more than sixty years until 1913, except for a short time between 1897 and 1899 when their financial solvency suffered a temporary lapse.

The relatively small Cota acreage was not suitable for extensive cattle ranching, but land along the creeks and the river supported diversified farming and sheep pasture during the changeable climate period of the 1860s and 1870s.

After Leonardo died in 1887, his son Guillermo José (1856–1941), always known as G.J., assumed leadership of the family, retaining the adobe as headquarters. The G.J. Cota family maintained a respectable position within the growing community at Rincon and in nearby Corona. G.J. had begun his community involvement by staying on the family ranch with his brother Teofilo after his father's death. Catholic Mass was held at the adobe before 1898, when a parish was established at Corona.

G.J. Cota moved his family to Corona in 1908, and his sister Maria Jesusa continued to occupy the adobe for a few more years. The third generation completely assimilated into the larger community of Corona. Having started school at Rincon, the younger children completed their last years in Corona. All the children had Anglicized nicknames, which were used in place of their more formal Spanish given names. Furthermore, all the children married into more recently arrived families with Anglo surnames.

Historic Bandini-Cota Adobe

The Bandini-Cota Adobe site on El Rincón grant is at the edge of a mesa above the Santa Ana River, which in 1941 became part of the flood basin of Prado Dam, not quite high enough to be immune from flooding during the most severe ravages of the river.

After the family finally left in 1913, an evaluation several years later found the house in reasonably good, very restorable condition. Photographs from 1926 and 1932 show its use for hay storage with an

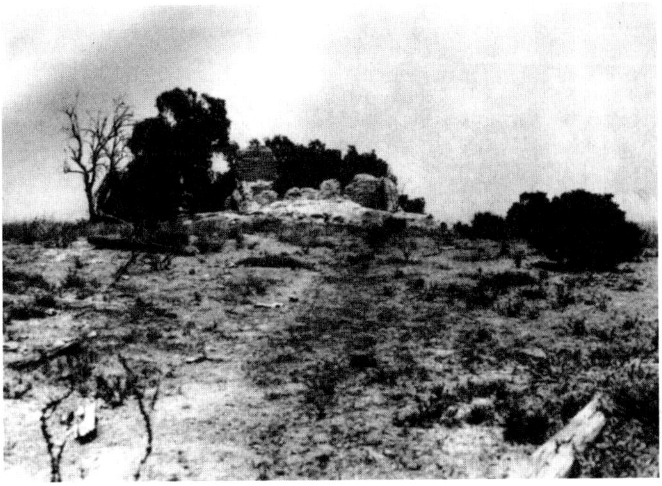

Ruins of the Bandini-Cota Adobe can still be identified on satellite maps. *Courtesy Steve Lech.*

attached corral. The roof remained mostly intact until 1938, when sale to Orange County Flood Control District was finalized. After that time, no further building maintenance appears to have been undertaken. The roof deteriorated, the exterior wall plaster scaled off and the structural adobe gradually dissolved.

By 1971, the walls had melted from their original two-story height to about seven feet, and deterioration continued to accelerate. Recent online satellite photos still reveal stubs of some of the walls, obviously consistent with previously published photos and drawings. The site is now surrounded by a fence and a few trees at the end of a restricted road in Riverside County, about two miles north of Prado Dam.

Chapter 2

TRANSITION: MEXICAN LAND GRANT RANCHES TO YANKEE FARMS

During the last half of the nineteenth century, the United States finally achieved its "manifest destiny," spreading across the entire North American continent to the Pacific Ocean. But this achievement did not come easily. Mexico had to be convinced, the hard way, to give up its claim to a vast expanse of land west of the Louisiana Purchase and south of Oregon, in exchange for a few million dollars.

Almost simultaneous with settlement of the Mexican War in 1848 was the discovery of gold in northern California, followed by California statehood in 1850. Thousands of immigrants arrived by long sea voyages or by wagon train across hundreds of miles of mountains and deserts.

A new era was dawning in Southern California. The sun was rising over the eastern mountains, but most rancho land titles still lay in legal shadows that finally brightened three decades later. Between 1870 and 1880, many former Mexican land grant titles in the southland were finally validated. Almost all landowners within the present-day city boundaries of Eastvale can trace their deeds back to 1879, the year when Jurupa grant was confirmed.

And between 1876 and 1905, four transcontinental railroad routes to Southern California were completed, greatly facilitating immigration of farmers eager to purchase newly available land.

2.1 The Mexican War (1846–1848)

Mexico Insists on Texas Claim: "Remember the Alamo"

After Mexico won independence from Spain in 1821, internal political turmoil continued. But politicians in Mexico City were unanimous regarding the status of Texas during the following decades. They overwhelmingly supported their country's claim to land north of the Rio Grande as Mexico's legitimate territory on historical grounds, despite increasing pressure from Yankee immigrants for independence or United States annexation. The same issue eventually echoed beyond Texas, throughout the region west of the Louisiana Purchase and south of Oregon Territory—a vast region that included California, and present-day Eastvale in particular.

The Battle of the Alamo, near present-day San Antonio, ended on 6 March 1836 with total defeat for the Texans, but Mexico's victory celebration was short-lived. At San Jacinto six weeks later on 21 April, Texan troops led by General Samuel Houston defeated a larger army under Mexican general Santa Anna and forced him to sign a treaty recognizing the Rio Grande as the southwestern boundary of Texas.

Mexico City never accepted the April 1836 treaty as valid, but the United States deemed it fully effective. Early the following year, President Andrew Jackson recognized Texas as an independent Lone Star Republic, over the strenuous objection of Mexico, which continued to insist that its northern boundaries extended far north of the Rio Grande. Mexico threatened war in response to America's next step: annexation of Texas into the United States as a state in 1845.

Manifest Destiny: "From Sea to Shining Sea"

The Doctrine of Manifest Destiny spread throughout the United States during the 1840s. This principle was based on a *manifest* (i.e., obvious) idea, that it was the *destiny* of the United States to expand westward across North America, all the way to the Pacific Ocean. Some versions of the doctrine were bold enough to apply it to the entire continent, extending southward to encompass all of Mexico and northward to include the British territories of Oregon and Canada.

Serious proposals were made for Mexico to cede California to the United States in settlement of debts or to arrange a settlement of ongoing

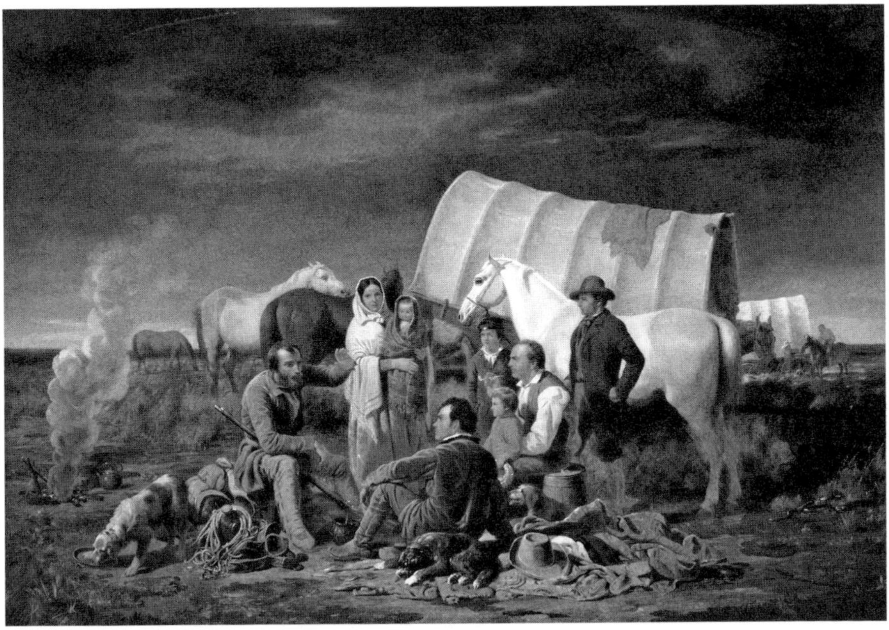

Immigrants came west across hundreds of miles of mountains and deserts. *Advice on the Prairie*, painting by William Tylee Ranney. *Courtesy Buffalo Bill Historical Center, Cody, WY.*

disputes with England concerning the Oregon territory, which meanwhile had been the subject of extensive exploration and colonization by Americans. The Oregon Trail was pioneered in 1836, and its branches to inland valleys of northern California were in use by 1843. Swiss immigrant John Augustus Sutter constructed his fort on the Sacramento River between 1841 and 1843.

Immigration from the eastern United States to California was a trickle compared to Texas and Oregon, but it had increased since Mexican independence, as restrictions from the Spanish regime were relaxed. Mexican land grants still locked up the coastal farmlands of California at least as far north as Monterey, as well as desirable inland regions including the Santa Ana River Valley and present-day Eastvale.

War Between the United States and Mexico, 1846

War between the United States and Mexico was finally triggered by a seemingly minor question as to whether the Texas-Mexico border was along the Rio Grande or some 150 miles farther northeast where a line had once been drawn at the Nueces River. On 25 April 1846, President James K. Polk provocatively sent General Zachary Taylor, with a large troop of soldiers, south past the Nueces River. Mexican troops responded northward across the Rio Grande. A history by Kennedy describes events of the war during 1846 and 1847:

> *Americans, especially southwestern expansionists, were eager to teach the Mexicans a lesson. The Mexicans, in turn, were burning to humiliate the "Bullies of the North."*
>
> *American operations in the Southwest and in California were completely successful. In 1846 General Stephen W. Kearny led a detachment of seventeen hundred troops over the famous Santa Fe Trail from Fort Leavenworth* [in northeastern Kansas] *to Santa Fe. This sun-baked outpost, with its drowsy plazas, was easily captured. But before Kearny could reach California, the fertile province was won.*
>
> *When war broke out, Captain John C. Frémont, the dashing explorer, just "happened" to be there* [at Sonoma, north of San Francisco] *with several dozen well-armed men. In helping to overthrow Mexican rule* [over California] *in 1846, he collaborated with American naval officers and with the local Americans, who had hoisted the banner of the short-lived California Bear Flag Republic.*
>
> *General Zachary Taylor meanwhile had been spearheading the main thrust across the Rio Grande into Mexico. After several gratifying victories, he reached Buena Vista* [near Monterrey in northern Mexico]. *There, on February 22–23, 1847, his weakened force of five thousand men was attacked by twenty thousand march-weary troops under Santa Anna. The Mexicans were finally repulsed with extreme difficulty.*

American strategy now called for an attack, which began with a landing at Veracruz, on the Gulf of Mexico 250 miles east of Mexico City. General Winfield Scott made a three-pronged advance on the capital, one of the most brilliant campaigns in American military annals. The Mexican army was overwhelmed, and Santa Anna surrendered.

Treaty of Guadalupe-Hidalgo, 1848

The Treaty of Guadalupe-Hidalgo was signed on 2 February 1848, at the Basilica of Guadalupe, a shrine that still exists at Villa Hidalgo in Mexico City.

The United States agreed to pay $15 million, in exchange for which Mexico relinquished territory known as the Mexican Cession, more than a half million square miles in extent. The treaty also confirmed the Rio Grande as the boundary between Texas and Mexico.

Mexican Cession land included the present-day states of California, Nevada and Utah, plus almost all of Arizona and parts of Montana,

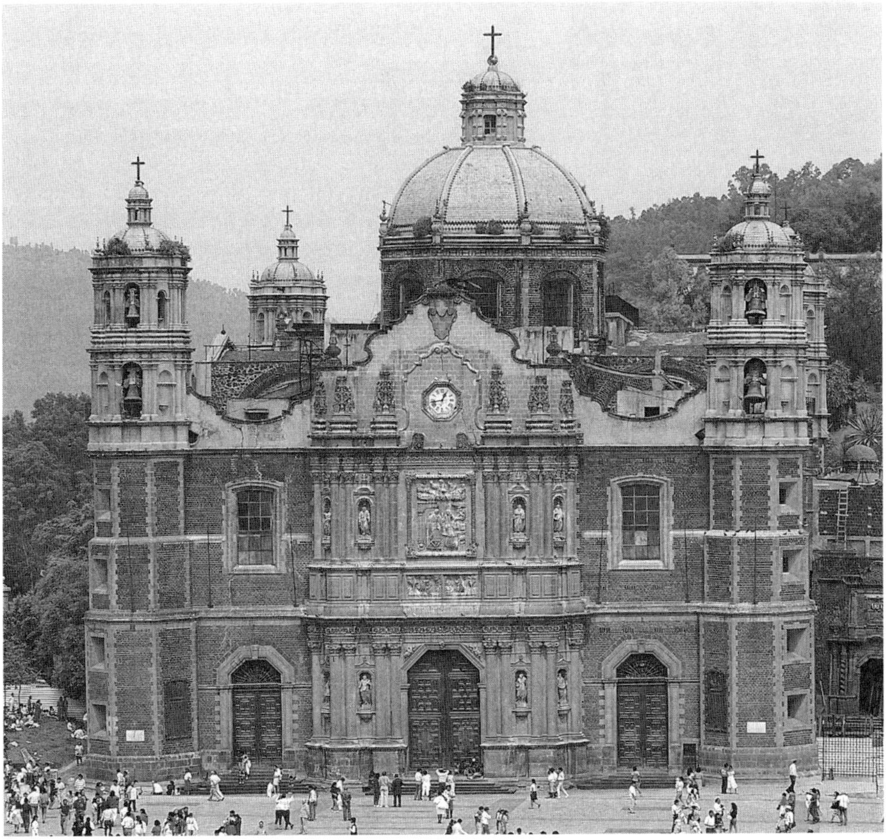

Basilica of Guadalupe, at Villa Hidalgo in present-day Mexico City, where the 1848 treaty was signed. *Courtesy DeAgostini Editore, Novara, Italy.*

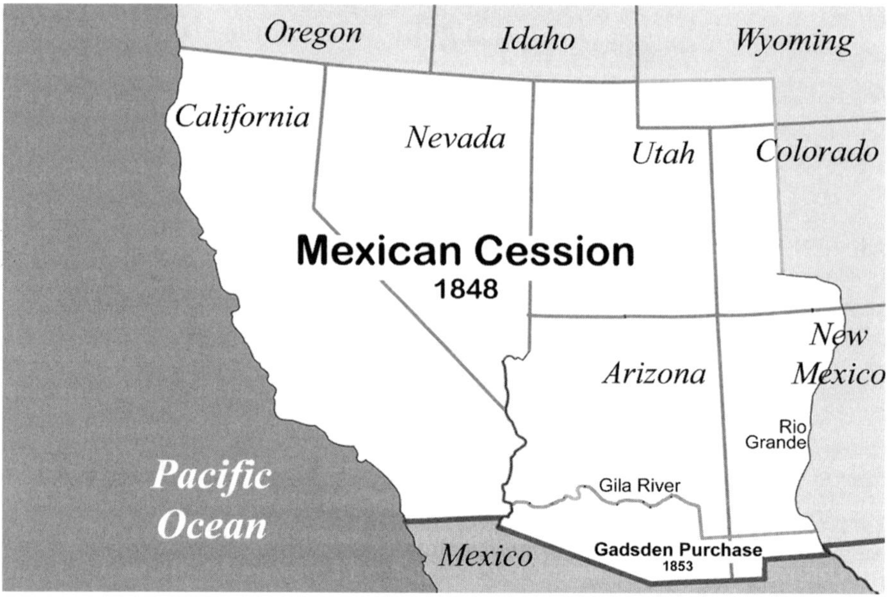

The Mexican Cession included three western U.S. states and parts of four others. Map reconstructed by Loren Meissner.

Colorado and New Mexico. The treaty completed present-day boundaries of the contiguous United States, except for the Gadsden Purchase in 1853, which added land to Arizona south of the Gila River.

2.2 "California, Here I Come" (1848–1870)

"I Have Found It!"

Mexico would likely have been even more reluctant to cede California to the United States on 2 February 1848 if it had been aware of an event in the northern part of the state only nine days earlier. On 24 January, James Marshall had noticed some shiny flecks in the tailrace of Sutter's sawmill on the American River. Marshall's recollection is reported at the Malakoff website:

> *I picked up one or two pieces and examined them attentively; and having some general knowledge of minerals, I could not call to mind more than two which*

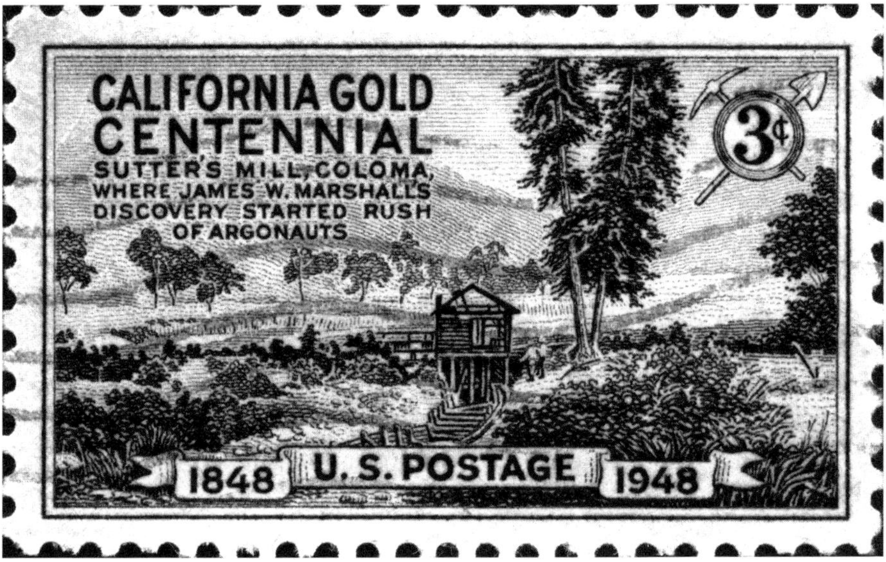

An estimated three hundred thousand immigrants came to California between 1848 and 1855. Stamp issued 1948. *Courtesy U.S. Post Office Department.*

> *in any way resembled this, sulphuret of iron* [probably iron sulfite, also called iron pyrite or fool's gold], *very bright and brittle; and gold, bright, yet malleable. I then tried it between two rocks, and found that it could be beaten into a different shape, but not broken. I then collected four or five pieces and went up to Mr. Scott (who was working at the carpenters bench making the mill wheel) with the pieces in my hand and said, "I have found it."*
>
> *"What is it?" inquired Scott.*
>
> *"Gold," I answered.*
>
> *"Oh! no," replied Scott, "That can't be."*
>
> *I said,—"I know it to be nothing else."*

The earliest gold seekers were American and European farmers already living in California. These were soon followed by Oregonians and by arrivals by sea from points farther south along the Pacific Coast and from the Sandwich Islands (Hawaii).

Within ten months, by the beginning of 1849, word of the gold rush had spread around the world. It is estimated that at least 300,000 gold seekers, merchants and other immigrants came to California between 1849 and 1855, about half of them having come from the eastern United States by land or sea.

Cattle Drives

Food was scarce at the gold mines because workers preferred to look for gold rather than till the soil, so cattle were driven to the gold country from the ranchos of Southern California. In the spring of 1849, Hugo Reid, whom Cleland describes as a picturesque and capricious Scotsman of San Gabriel, suggested to Abel Stearns that he should take advantage of the financial opportunity presented by the market for beef in the north. By this time, the astute Don Abel had become owner or administrator of most of the land grant territory in the San Gabriel and Santa Ana River Valleys. Some of the meat that filled the bellies of Forty-niners undoubtedly came from cattle that were driven north from grassland sites in present-day Eastvale.

This temporary windfall for the Dons had longer-lasting repercussions. The gold rush created an enormous and ever-expanding demand for beef, raised the price of cattle to levels never before dreamed of in California, destroyed the simple scale of values to which the ranchers had long been accustomed and transformed herds of black, slim-bodied cattle into far richer bonanzas than the gold fields of the Sierra yielded to a vast majority of the Argonauts. The long-established custom of slaughtering cattle for hides and tallow rapidly gave place to the much more profitable business of selling the animals for beef.

Aftermath

As the more accessible gold deposits were depleted, some miners returned to their former homes in the eastern United States, but the vast majority remained in California. Some continued mining with more elaborate machinery, while others became farmers, merchants, mechanics or workers in a variety of other fields. California was still isolated from the rest of the United States by hundreds of miles of deserts and mountains, but its population continued to increase. The population of California, according to the U.S. Census Bureau, was 93,000 in 1850; 380,000 in 1860; 560,000 in 1870; 864,000 in 1880; 1,213,000 in 1890; and 1,485,000 in 1900.

Even without the gold discovery, California statehood would undoubtedly have been inevitable soon after annexation by the United States. But the political process was accelerated by the resulting influx of population, which also created a need for institutions to assist and protect the new citizens. Despite some objection from southerners in Congress to the admission of a new free state, California became the thirty-first state on 9 September 1850.

"Respect" for Mexican Land Titles?

The Treaty of Guadalupe-Hidalgo expressed intent to respect Mexican-era landownership, but later modifications and interpretations of the treaty did not conform consistently to this assurance. The U.S. Congress insisted on strict standards for patenting (examining and certifying) Mexican-era land titles. Chapter 1 has noted that documentation of boundaries in the earlier era was often nonexistent or, at best, vague. For example, distances were typically based on the length of a rawhide cord "one hundred *varas* long" that could stretch or shrink with temperature, humidity or rough handling.

In later years, some of the more successful challenges in land grant cases were based on homestead claims by former residents of the eastern United States who had the foresight to maintain careful land measurements and records. U.S. land commissions and courts may have been biased in favor of Yankees accused of "squatting"—taking possession of land they did not own—but this seems to have been infrequent in El Rincón and in the portion of Jurupa that was deeded to Abel Stearns in 1859, including present-day Eastvale.

As soon as California became a state, serious steps were taken to begin verifying and settling land claims. Surveys made during 1852 established Principal Meridians at Mount San Bernardino for Southern California and at Mount Diablo for central California. Township survey lines were laid out six miles apart, according to the scheme that had been applied in all accessible parts of the United States west of the Appalachian Mountains, usually before each region became populated.

The U.S. Public Lands Commission, created to determine the validity of Spanish and Mexican land grants, confirmed most California claims between 1851 and 1856. However, in land grant regions along the central California coast, and in the southern coastal and inland valleys, many titles were not finally patented until the 1870s or later. Statehood provided increased incentive for immigration to California, but uncertainty of land titles remained a serious obstacle to landownership.

The 1860s: End of an Era

During the 1860s, most of the United States was focusing attention on the War Between the States and its aftermath, the Reconstruction era. By comparison, California's involvement in the Civil War was mostly indirect: sending gold east, recruiting volunteer combat units to replace regular forces in territories of the western United States, maintaining and building numerous camps and fortifications, suppressing secessionist activity and securing the New Mexico Territory against the Confederacy. At the end of the war, displaced Southerners added to population pressure and to discontent with the unsettled situation concerning former Mexican land titles.

The big news of the decade in California, however, was the plight of the Dons. For the most part, they had not yet succeeded in clearing title to their grants, even after considerable expenditures for land surveys and documentation review, exacerbated by exorbitant legal fees and high interest rates on the resulting obligations, all of which had brought many of them close to bankruptcy.

But the worst was yet to come.

Puntney describes weather problems during the 1860s with specific reference to the Robidoux section of Jurupa. But his report applies almost equally to other parts of the grant during the same years, including present-day Eastvale, and in large measure to most of Southern California.

> *On November 11, 1861 it began to rain in California. It rained, almost without ceasing, through Thanksgiving. Then, for four weeks, the storms abated. The rain began again on Christmas Eve and continued through January 1862. On Friday, January 31, William Brewer wrote: "At Los Angeles it rained incessantly for twenty eight days—one whole village destroyed. It is supposed that over one-fourth of the taxable property has been destroyed."*
>
> [In the Santa Ana River Valley,] *the waters which freight-trained through the villages carried away their homes, fences, even their fields, leaving, in their stead, only sterile sand and a hideous plain of black boulders and cobblestones.*
>
> *Below, Robidoux' bottomland fields were also destroyed. The mill* [near Redlands]...*was gone and its millrace filled with river sand. Only the two heavy lava millstones remained to show where it once had stood.*
>
> *In the spring of 1862 things began to look up. The heavy rains of a few months before resulted in a good range for the cattle. They fattened on the rich grass and brought the best prices in years. But the return of good times was transitory. When the skies cleared in January 1862, they remained clear for more than two years.*
>
> *The drought went unrelieved from January 1862, until February 1864, and continued intermittently through the better part of the decade.*

> *Historian Leonard Pitt has judged that it was "a physical disaster as great as if California had stood in the path of Sherman's march to the sea." Cattle died by the thousands; only their hides could sometimes be saved for market. Vineyards and orchards withered. Field crops failed. In the face of all this, Louis Robidoux was brought to the edge of ruin. In 1865, a year of passable rain, he began to sell the lands of his rancho.*
>
> *It signaled the end of an era.* [Other farmers] *would come but it would never be the same. The Rancho Jurupa was gone and as it passed so passed the rancho system.*

Irrigation finally eased the threat of disastrous droughts, beginning about twenty years later with the Gage Canal in 1886, supplemented with newly invented pumps driven by petroleum fuels or by electricity from evolving distribution systems. Flooding was still a serious threat for farms close to the river until much later, when dams were constructed near Eastvale at Prado in 1941 and upstream at Seven Oaks in 1999.

Mexican Ranchos Become Yankee Farms

The end of the rancho era was heavily influenced by another factor. Many land patents were settled during the 1870s, meaning that owners of grant land now had firm legal titles. For the first time since the Guadalupe-Hidalgo Treaty in 1848, their land was a solid economic asset. Jurupa-Robidoux, the eastern 15 percent of Bandini's Jurupa grant, was patented in 1876, and Jurupa-Stearns, the western 85 percent of Jurupa, was patented in 1879.

The Jurupa-Stearns 1879 patent included the present-day city of Eastvale, except for small acreages of city territory at the northeast corner (north of Bellegrave) and at the southwest corner (west of Hellman) that had always been outside Jurupa grant boundaries. This 1879 title settlement finally resolved provisions in the Treaty of Guadalupe-Hidalgo for this part of Jurupa grant and thus became the ultimate basis of landownership for almost all present-day Eastvale residents.

As may be recalled from Chapter 1, Juan Bandini had held this western 85 percent of Jurupa until he transferred it to Abel Stearns in 1859 to clear his mortgage. Meanwhile, Stearns had died in 1871, and the title passed to his wife, Arcadia. The neighboring El Rincón grant was also patented in 1879, to Bernardo Yorba, confirming the validity of intervening transfers including the Bandini-Cota Adobe site.

Stearns was hit hard by the drought of 1863–64, causing the loss of thousands of cattle. By 1868, Stearns had suffered such financial reverses that he mortgaged all his ranch assets in what were then Los Angeles and San Bernardino Counties. To obtain the necessary operating capital, he formed a real estate sales partnership with Alfred Robinson and four San Francisco investors. As Cleland points out:

> [Between 1848 and 1870,] *most of the great land holdings in southern California passed from the control of native Californians into the hands of Americans. The change was inevitable. It was brought about by the Land Act of 1851* [implementing provisions of the Treaty of Guadalupe-Hidalgo], *whose harmful and confusing effects upon the old Spanish-Mexican titles have already been described; by the prodigality, extravagance, and financial ineptitude of the native Californians; by inequitable short-term mortgages and fantastically high interest rates; by a prolonged depression in the cattle industry, following a period of skyrocketing prices produced by the Gold Rush; and, finally, by the historic drought of the mid-sixties, which caused a wide-spread revolution in the life and customs of southern California.*

The entire concept behind the rancho system had become tiresomely out of date. Cattle raising on large spreads of land had started long before as an occupational outlet for the Mission Indians, rewarded by the exchange of hides and tallow for imported necessities and luxuries from ships that occasionally visited the coast. In the meantime, the custom of discarding most of the beef (mainly because of the difficulty of preserving it) had changed, since there were now more local residents who might purchase meat products for immediate consumption. Soil exhaustion due to monoculture (a concept unknown or at least unnamed in 1870) was no doubt another factor. Irrigation for the large stretches of land involved had not yet been developed.

Simply stated, large-scale cattle ranching, as it had been practiced for almost one hundred years in most of California's coastal and inland valleys, no longer made sense. But until the land patent settlements, it had been difficult to convert ranch grant land to other uses.

The viewpoint of small farmers who came to California before 1875 was recalled in 1890 by Van Dyke:

> *From 1870 to 1875, Southern California was passing out of the control of the large land owners, nearly all of whom* [had been] *raising cattle,*

> *horses, and sheep to the exclusion of anything else, and into the control of the general farmer and fruit grower.*
>
> *There was an attraction about the soft climate of winter and the dry, cool sea-breeze of summer, in the long line of sunny days with nights made for soundest sleep, and in the absence of storms, high winds, and other climatic discomforts, that made people stay, however unsuccessful, and steadily brought more to stay with them. It was a grand play-country, and one could get along with less than in any other part of the United States and still be respectable and fat. But everywhere there was a broad smile when some enthusiastic newcomer said that it would some day be the richest part of the United States outside the great cities.*

As soon as titles to the land were secure, it could be subdivided and sold at a fair price to individual farmers who had recently come to California, in plots of a square mile or less, even as small as forty acres. The Dons could sell farm plots and use the proceeds to settle the debts they had accrued in defending their titles, with some profit to compensate for losses they had incurred due to the weather ravages of the previous decade. The era of the large cattle ranchos was on the way out. In its place came agriculture, as ranchos were broken up and generally sold in forty-acre farms and ranches. By 1870, Stearns was out from under the debts incurred by the drought of the 1860s and was on his way to accumulating yet another fortune. But, before he could realize that fortune, Abel Stearns died.

What Comes Next?

So there was now ample land for sale, but a question remained. Would potential buyers keep coming to California, across the many hundreds of miles of mountains and deserts?

A new sound heard in the distance might bring the answer. It was a train whistle.

2.3 Impact of the Railroads (1870–1900)

"Go West, Young Man"

Everyone has heard of the Golden Spike ceremony at Promontory, Utah, on 10 May 1869, joining the westbound Union Pacific Railroad from Omaha, Nebraska, with the eastbound Central Pacific from Sacramento. This ceremony celebrated the final link in the first rail connection from the Great Plains to California—although coast-to-coast travel entirely by rail was still not quite possible until a few loose ends, such as river crossings by ferry, were tied down a year or so later.

It was railroads that made the new era in California a success. At first, transcontinental railroads were viewed as a means for bringing people and cargo from the eastern United States to California, but they soon proved equally suitable for transporting agricultural and other goods from the productive land of California to markets in the East.

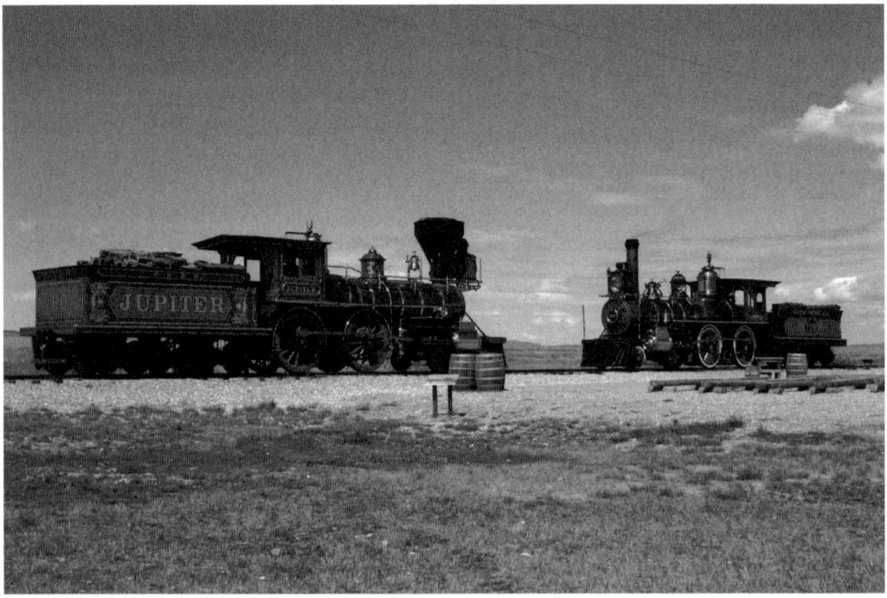

On 10 May 1869, a Golden Spike connected the eastern U.S. with California by rail. The 1869 ceremony is reenacted every year on the 10 May anniversary, as well as every Saturday and holiday from May to September, with replicas of the original locomotives, Central Pacific No. 60 (Jupiter) and Union Pacific No. 119. *Courtesy National Park Service.*

To Los Angeles—But via Sacramento?

Sacramento and San Francisco were logical choices as western terminals for the first rails across the continent. Before 1870, California's population growth focused in the north. The gold rush attracted immigrants northward, while Southern California retained a rancho legacy that did not encourage large numbers of small landowners.

But Southern California's star was rising. Terminals on railroads from the eastern United States existed, or were soon anticipated, at Salt Lake City, Albuquerque and El Paso, but the decision was made to postpone construction of a new direct line to Los Angeles from those points, any of which would require laying new rails across six hundred miles or more of desert. Instead, the initial project would be a connection from northern California and the Golden Spike route.

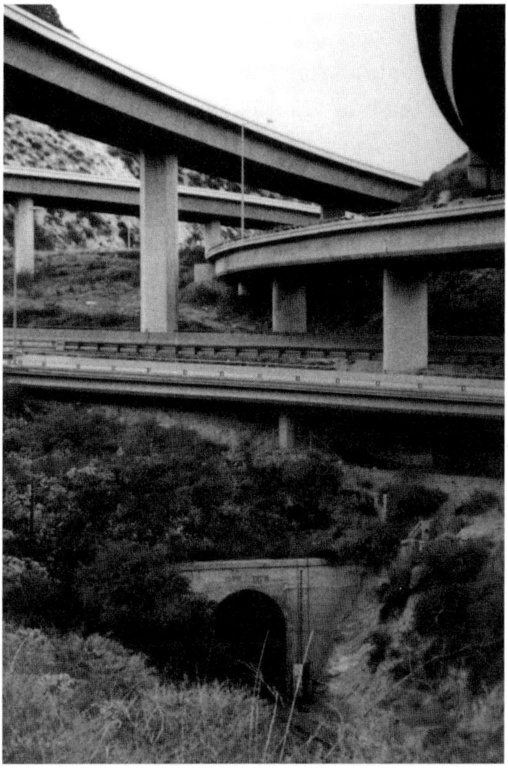

San Fernando Tunnel between San Fernando and Santa Clarita, completed almost 150 years ago, now serves the Metrolink commuter line between Los Angeles and Antelope Valley. The southern portal is almost hidden underneath a major freeway interchange known affectionately as the "bowl of worms." Photo by Jann Mayer. *Courtesy Bridgehunter.*

By 1874, the Southern Pacific Railroad, a subsidiary of Central Pacific, had extended service from northern California through the Central Valley, as far south as Bakersfield. And railroad construction was already underway for the remaining 150-mile stretch from Bakersfield to Los Angeles—over, around and through the mountains via Tehachapi, Mojave and Palmdale.

There were two major obstacles between Bakersfield and Los Angeles.

The Tehachapi Mountains, a spur at the southern end of the Sierra Nevada, had to be traversed east of Bakersfield over a pass at almost 4,000 feet elevation. On the west side, between Bakersfield and the summit, the last nine miles of the route rose 1,200 feet, which implied a 2.5 percent gradient—half a percent too steep for optimal mainline rail freight requirements.

The solution designed by Southern Pacific engineer William Hood was the Tehachapi Loop, completed in 1876, which curves a section of track back to cross itself, reducing the grade by adding almost another mile of length. Even today, visitors are frequently fortunate enough to watch a mile-long eastbound train traversing the loop, with the locomotive crossing seventy-seven feet above its rear cars in the tunnel below as the train gains elevation around the central hill of the loop.

The second obstacle was just north of Los Angeles. The pass between San Fernando and Palmdale goes through a low but steep ridge at the west end of the San Gabriel Mountain range. A straight 1.3-mile-long tunnel was constructed to carry the railroad track through the ridge. At the time of its completion in 1876, this was the third-longest tunnel in the United States.

Very soon after the loop and tunnel established the Southern Pacific Railroad link between Bakersfield and Los Angeles, a celebration was held at Lang, twenty-five miles southwest of Palmdale. On 5 September 1876, about seven years after the 1869 Golden Spike ceremony, the rail connection was complete from the eastern United States via Sacramento, southward through California's Central Valley to Bakersfield, eastward to Mojave and southward into Los Angeles.

Major Rail Links before 1900

Along the East Coast and through the Mississippi Valley, railroad lines had spread with few restrictions across plains and low mountain ranges. A few routes were in place as early as 1830, and more were built after the Railroad Land Grant Act of 1850.

Between the Great Plains and the West Coast, however, a relief map of the United States shows very few feasible railroad routes through the mountains. From northern California, there are only two rail routes to Nevada across the Sierra Nevada and Cascade mountain ranges—the Golden Spike route via Donner Pass, and Beckworth Pass, which was developed much later along the Feather River.

Similarly, only three mountain passes are available for rails connecting Los Angeles directly to points farther east: Newhall Pass from San

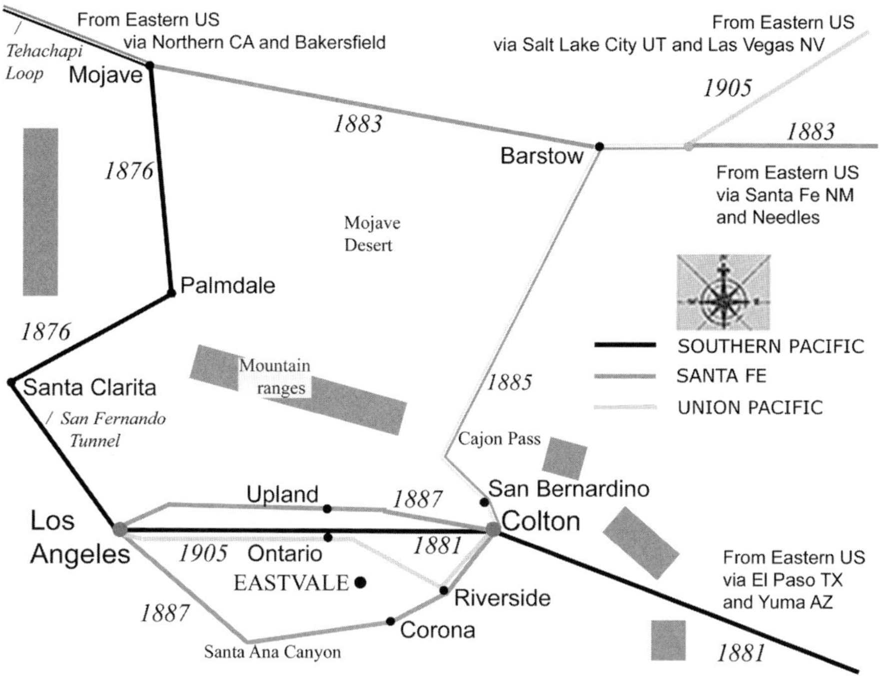

Railroads to Los Angeles from the eastern United States were completed via northern California in 1876, via El Paso, Texas, in 1881; via Santa Fe, New Mexico, in 1883; and via Salt Lake City, Utah, in 1905. Map by Loren Meissner.

Fernando to Santa Clarita and Palmdale, San Gorgonio Pass from Colton to Palm Springs and Yuma and Cajon Pass from San Bernardino to Barstow. These three routes were exploited by 1887, six years before Riverside County was formed. Transcontinental railroad lines connected Southern California with the eastern United States—over Newhall Pass from northern California in 1876; through San Gorgonio Pass from El Paso, Texas, in 1881; and via Barstow and Cajon Pass from Santa Fe, New Mexico, in 1885.

Principal routes, in order of their completion, are as follows:

In 1876, the Southern Pacific Railroad, meeting its connection from the eastern United States at Sacramento, connected via Bakersfield, the Tehachapi Loop, Mojave, Palmdale and the San Fernando Tunnel into Los Angeles.

In 1881, the Southern Pacific Railroad linked the southeastern United States via El Paso, Texas; Yuma, Arizona; Palm Springs; San Gorgonio Pass; and Colton to Los Angeles. This Yuma line proposal had been an important incentive for the 1853 Gadsden Purchase, but construction was postponed because of pre–Civil War politics.

In 1883, the Santa Fe Railroad connected Santa Fe, New Mexico, and points farther east with Mojave via Needles and Barstow. Santa Fe shared Southern Pacific tracks over Tehachapi Pass to connect Mojave with Bakersfield and northern California. This Santa Fe line was targeted toward Bakersfield and did not yet continue into Los Angeles, but it provided a link to Southern Pacific at Mojave.

In 1885, California Southern Railroad completed the route over Cajon Pass from Barstow to Colton. In 1887, Santa Fe took over California Southern routes and constructed two lines between Colton and Los Angeles, via Upland and through Santa Ana Canyon. This Santa Ana Canyon line proved advantageous in the development of ranches and farms near present-day Eastvale and Corona.

After 1900: Salt Lake City to Los Angeles (Union Pacific)

There was still no direct railroad link to Southern California from the 1869 Golden Spike route near Salt Lake City. A route from Utah through Las Vegas would be two hundred miles shorter, and less vulnerable to weather, than over the Sierra Nevada via Donner Pass to Sacramento, continuing south through Bakersfield and Mojave.

Surveys along the Salt Lake route, and construction of short sections, date from about 1880. The proposed eight-hundred-mile route approximated the present-day Interstate Highway 15 alignment from the Central Pacific rail junction at Ogden, Utah, southward through Salt Lake City, Las Vegas, Barstow and Cajon Pass, to Colton and Riverside.

In 1900, U.S. senator William A. Clark of Montana, a celebrated mining speculator, newspaper publisher, politician, railroad builder and capitalist, formed a corporation to undertake construction of a "Salt Lake Route." But E.H. Harriman, of Union Pacific Railroad, which had been the eastern participant in the Golden Spike project, already had his sights set on a similar route. In a series of compromises and transactions described in books by Signor and by Asay, Clark constructed most of the route between Ogden and Los Angeles and then traded his share of Salt Lake Route ownership for Union Pacific stock.

In 1905, rails from Ogden and Salt Lake City reached the 1883 Santa Fe line at Daggett, California, about ten miles east of Barstow. From Daggett

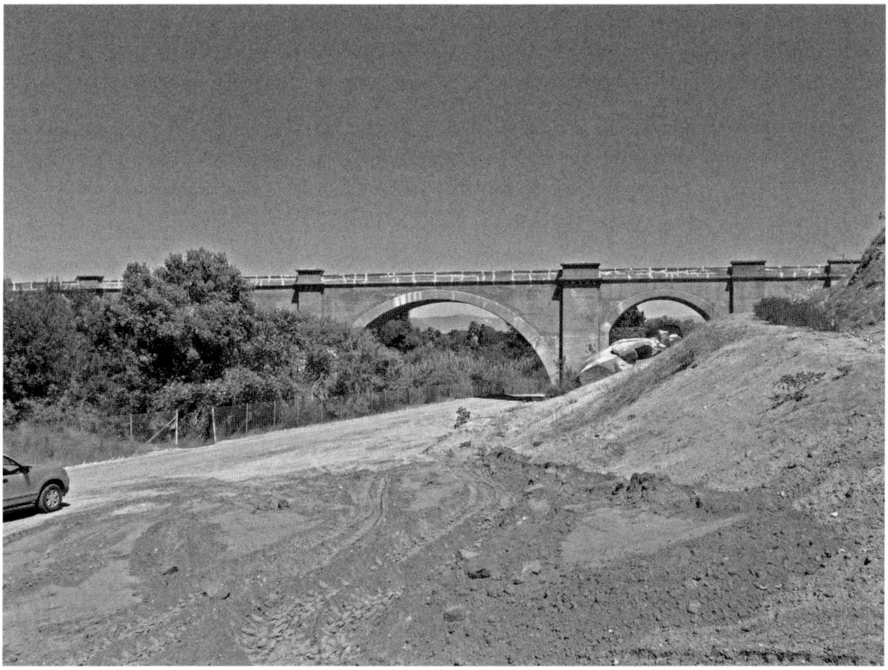

Union Pacific Railroad bridge at Pedley near Eastvale, constructed 1902–04. Loren Meissner photo, 2012.

over Cajon Pass to Riverside, Clark arranged to share Santa Fe tracks. Meanwhile, Clark had also constructed tracks from Los Angeles to Riverside through Ontario and Pedley (in present-day Jurupa Valley). This Union Pacific line, inaugurated with a "maiden voyage" in May 1905, reduced travel time between Salt Lake City and Los Angeles to one day.

Westbound trains leaving Riverside on the 1905 Union Pacific track still cross the Santa Ana River east of Van Buren Boulevard on a bridge built during the years 1902 to 1904. Costing several hundred thousand dollars, the Santa Ana River bridge was a ten-arch structure, close to one-fifth of a mile long and over sixty feet high. At the time of its construction, it held the title of the longest concrete arch bridge in the world.

The bridge site is known as De Anza Narrows, said to be the place where Juan Bautista de Anza crossed the Santa Ana River on his expeditions from Sonora, Mexico, in 1774 and 1776. The Union Pacific Railroad bridge near Pedley survived the March 1938 flood, when almost all highway bridges across the Santa Ana River, including the nearby Pedley Road bridge (near the present-day Van Buren Boulevard crossing), were swept away.

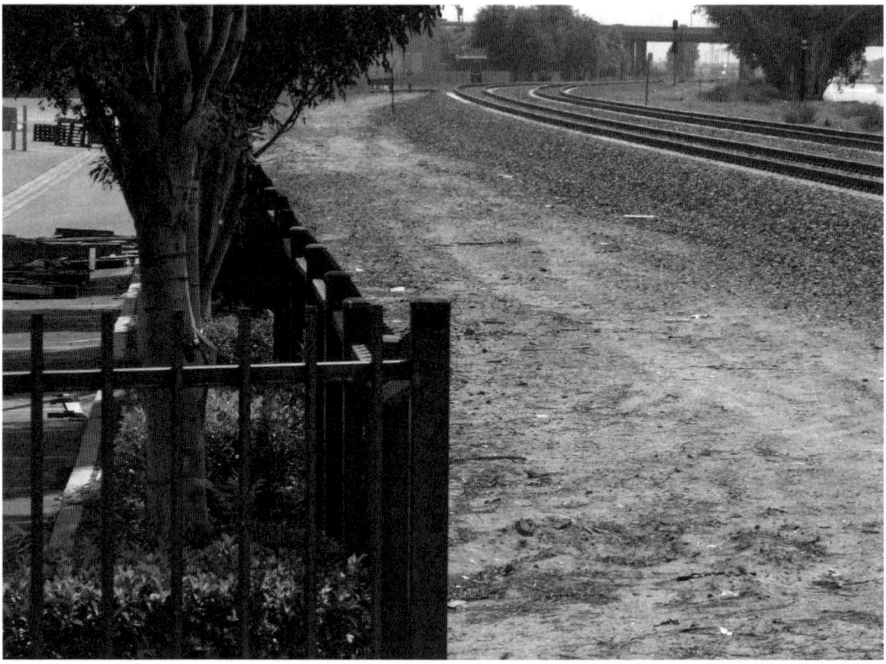

Between Interstate 15 and Milliken (Hamner) Avenue, about a half mile of mainline Union Pacific tracks pass through the north end of Eastvale. Loren Meissner photo, 2012.

The 1905 Union Pacific route, the fourth (and final) major rail route built across the Inland Empire region, intersects present-day Eastvale's "panhandle" north of U.S. Highway 60. The intersection consists of almost a half mile of mainline Union Pacific tracks between Interstate 15 and Milliken (Hamner) Avenue.

Present-Day Railroad Lines

Four main lines, constructed before 1905 by three railroad companies, are still in operation near Eastvale: The Southern Pacific line, completed in 1881, goes directly from Colton to Ontario, along the north side of present-day Ontario Airport. Santa Fe completed *two lines* from Colton in 1887: one through Cucamonga and Upland, and another via Corona and Santa Ana Canyon. Union Pacific in 1905 completed the line from Riverside via Pedley, across the Eastvale "panhandle" north of Mission Boulevard and along the south side of Ontario Airport.

Since World War II, many miles of railroad track have been abandoned as significant portions of their traffic shifted to faster airlines or more flexible surface road routes. The railroads still have a role carrying heavy long-distance freight, and some of the same roadbeds are still used for Amtrak transcontinental passenger service and for Metrolink commuter services.

Can You Hear It Now?

Loren clearly remembers, while growing up during the 1930s, lying in bed on quiet nights listening to sounds from across the open mesas. He often heard the whistle of Union Pacific trains as they approached the junction of Etiwanda Avenue and Mission Boulevard, about three miles north.

But nights are no longer so still, and the sound of the train whistle no longer carries so clearly through the clutter of buildings that occupy the plain. Another pleasure from a simpler era is lost.

2.4 Land Speculation (1880–1890)

A land boom that reached its peak about 1887 is the subject of a monograph written by Van Dyke in 1890. Although irrigation had already begun to increase the value of former Mexican grant land, the railroads were bringing large numbers of people to Southern California. Most of them were enchanted by the climate and the varied topography that featured seashores, mountains, rivers and plains. Land speculation was encouraged by promises of new cities whose predicted population exceeded the actual influx. But when the bubble burst, it turned out that the total amount invested did not exceed the intrinsic value of the land for irrigated farming.

Chapter 3

FULLER RANCH AT EASTVALE

The Fuller family owned a large ranch in present-day Eastvale for about sixty-five years, between 1889 and 1954. Surprisingly little is publicly known about this remarkable family, whose business projects were extremely successful during the early growth boom in Southern California before 1900. The Fuller Ranch illustrates some of the ways in which land title availability, railroad transportation and irrigation influenced development.

Harrison Fuller (1832–1903), patriarch of the family, was born in Pennsylvania, not far from a river resort named Eastvale, and he moved to Maryland at an early age. Between 1855 and 1883, he lived with his wife, Mary Ann, in Iowa, where the five youngest of their six children were born. In 1883, they moved from Iowa to Southern California. They settled on a farm at Azusa, about twenty-five miles northeast of downtown Los Angeles. Economic boom times were just beginning—largely in response to the recent completion of transcontinental railroad lines (see Chapter 2). Two sons, Charles Henry Fuller (1858–1929) and Ortus Benton Fuller (1865–1922), initiated many business ventures, several of which proved very successful. One of these was Pioneer Transfer Company, which provided local transportation for goods and people to and from railroad terminals in Los Angeles. Other successful undertakings included Fuller Department Stores, Los Angeles Warehouse Company and Enterprise Construction Company.

The brothers soon expanded into ranching in Eastvale and elsewhere. By 1889, they had enough money to buy a three-thousand-acre ranch (almost five square miles) near the Santa Ana River at present-day Eastvale. The

1897 JULIUS CAHN'S OFFICIAL THEATRICAL GUIDE 1897

LOS ANGELES, CAL.

(Pcpulation, 97,000.)

THEATRES.

Los Angeles Theatre	H. C. Wyatt, Mgr.
Orpheum	
Burbank Theatre	Fred. C. Cooper, Mgr.

NEWSPAPERS.

"Times" (daily and Sunday)	L. E. Mosher.
"Herald" (daily and Sunday)	Geo. Robinson.
"Journal" (daily and Sunday)	Warren Wilson.
"Eclipse" (daily, afternoon)	
"Express" (daily, afternoon)	Chas. F. Sloan.
"Record" (daily, afternoon)	Paul Beades.
"World" (Sunday)	E. F. Kubel.

HOTELS.

Van Nuys	$3.00 and up.
Hollenbeck	2.50 "
Nadeau	2.50 "
Westminster	2.50 "
Hoffman	$1.50 and $1.25
St. Elmo	1.50 and 1.25
Ramina	1.50 and 1.25

RAILROADS.

Southern Pacific	J. M. Crawley.
Santa Fé	H. Ruarles.
L. A. Terminal	W. Wurcup.
Pioneer Truck Company	
Express Co	Wells-Fargo.

C. H. FULLER. FRED ZUCKER.

Pioneer Truck and Transfer Co.

Theatrical Hauling a Specialty.

105 Market Street, - - Los Angeles, Cal.

HOTEL RAMONA,

LOS ANGELES, CAL.

Most centrally located. Nearest Theatres, etc. First-class, at moderate rates. New Sanitary Plumbing and Electric Bells. Special to Professionals. European plan, 50c. per day up; American plan, $1.50 and $1.75 up.

F. B. MALLORY, Proprietor.

Charles Fuller and his brother-in-law Fred Zucker advertised the services of their Pioneer Truck and Transfer Company in Julius Cahn's 1897 *Official Theatrical Guide. Courtesy Smithsonian Americana Collection.*

initial purpose of the Fuller brothers' Pioneer Ranch was to raise horses for their Los Angeles transportation business. Over the next forty years, the core of the ranch occupied most of the southern end of present-day Eastvale, from Schleisman Road south to the river, between Hellman Avenue and Hamner Avenue. The ranch was later augmented with two thousand leased acres of land in the river valley.

About 1900, the Fuller brothers' transportation business in Los Angeles was converted from horse-drawn wagons to motor trucks. An advertisement from 1897, at the bottom of a guide to Los Angeles theatrical entertainment, lists C.H. Fuller and his brother-in-law Fred Zucker as proprietors of Pioneer Truck and Transfer Company. Inclusion of the word "Truck" in the company name might be considered remarkable, since motor trucks had only recently been invented. This seems to illustrate the Fullers' willingness to accept technological innovations.

By 1907, the ranch at Eastvale had become known as one of the best cattle and racehorse breeding farms in California. Besides pasture for the horses, hogs and other livestock, large acreages were devoted to barley and alfalfa, much of which was exported, and to truck crops, including corn, melons and beets.

Between 1905 and 1920, the brothers had ranching subsidiaries in Santa Barbara County and Imperial County, California, "devoted exclusively to stock-raising, where are cattle, horses, and hogs by the thousands," according to the *Corona Daily Independent* of 3 May 1907. Some of these ranching ventures involved partnerships with the Hollister family, pioneers from northern California. Younger brother Ernest Pearl Fuller was overseer for distant family undertakings in Arizona, in Texas near El Paso and in Chihuahua, Mexico.

Ortus died 18 October 1922, and Charles's health failed about 1925. Olive Ransome Fuller, son of Charles, took over the Eastvale ranch.

Although the brothers sometimes leased land downriver in Orange County, they were *not* involved in founding Fullerton, as is sometimes claimed. The town was named for George H. Fullerton (1843–1929), a Santa Fe Railroad executive who chose the planned city site for a stop on the Santa Ana Canyon railroad line.

3.1 NEXT GENERATION: OLIVE RANSOME FULLER AND FULLER RANCHO

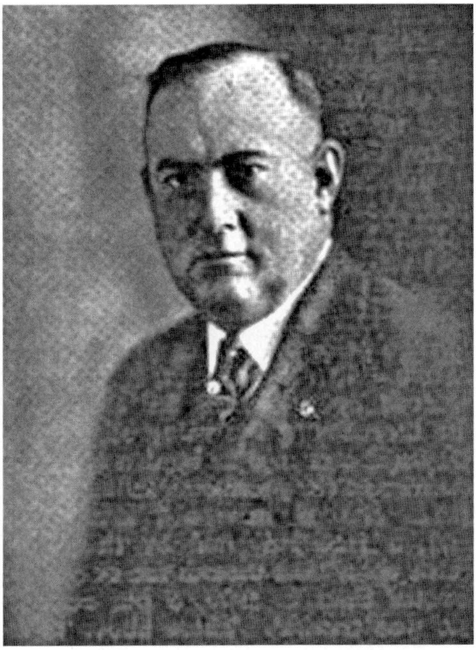

O.R. Fuller's role in Southern California bus transport was commended, as described in *Bus Transportation*, June 1922. *Courtesy McGraw-Hill.*

Olive Ransome Fuller (1880–1946) was always known as O.R. He was born in Iowa before the Fuller family moved to California. His father and his mother, Maud, separated soon after the boy was born. O.R. remained with his mother in the Midwest, and he didn't see his father again until he came to California when he was eighteen years old.

Between 1907 and 1929, O.R. Fuller was successful as a truck dealer and then as a motor transit manager. His name can be found in a number of specialized automobile dealership and bus transportation publications, including the trade periodical *Bus Transportation*, where an article in June 1922 praises him as a "Captain of Industry," especially because of his initiatives toward providing bus transportation throughout Southern California.

By 1916, streetcars were providing local passenger transportation within a few miles of downtown Los Angeles, but a more flexible plan was needed for longer distances, and O.R. Fuller formed Motor Transit Company to meet this need.

In 1921, the Motor Transit Company operated 6,058,285 passenger car miles. This service was rendered with about 130 cars of capacities ranging from eight to thirty-two passengers. The company's gross revenue for the year was $1,444,453, and a total of 2,152,988 passengers were carried in 1921. The combined lengths of the several routes traveled by the cars of this system total 800 miles.

Later, in 1929, O.R. Fuller sold Motor Transit Company to the Greyhound Bus Corporation for $3 million and went into business as a luxury car agent

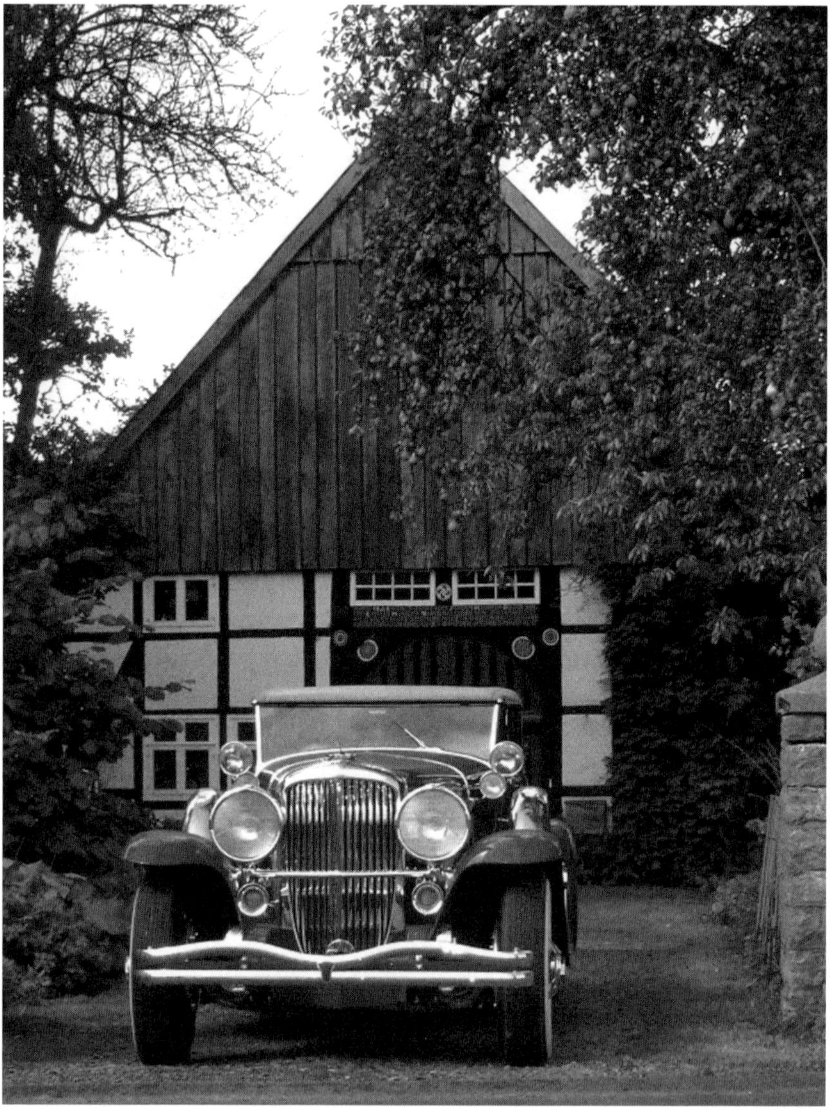

The historical birthplace of car builders Fred and August Deusenberg, at Kirchheide in the state of Bremen, Germany, hosts a 1929 Duesenberg J Murphy Convertible Coupe. *Courtesy Ulrich Schumacher.*

on Wilshire Boulevard in Los Angeles. His agency sold Auburn, Cord and Duesenberg cars, but its initial success was abruptly terminated after about two years by the Great Depression.

Marcellie's Story, 1931–1954

After O.R. Fuller's first wife, Agnes, died in 1918, childless, he married Ione Franklin. Marcellie, their only child, was born in Los Angeles in 1920.

Charles Fuller, father of O.R., owned the ranch at Eastvale after his brother Ortus died in 1922. When Charles's health failed about 1925, O.R. took control of the ranch, and in 1928, he built an elegant weekend retreat he called Casa Orone (a merger of the names of O.R. and his wife, Ione).

Then the Depression arrived. O.R. Fuller's tenure as a luxury car dealer was short-lived. When his car business failed in 1931, his only remaining asset was his weekend resort at Eastvale.

Marcellie takes up the narrative in her oral history, which was recorded in 1983 and is on file at Corona Public Library in the Heritage collection.

O.R. moved to the Eastvale ranch with Ione and their eleven-year-old daughter. Marcellie attended junior high and high school at Pomona, where her father set up business headquarters for the dairy he established on the Eastvale ranch. The dairy was a successful venture, with milk deliveries soon offered throughout Cucamonga Valley. O.R. Fuller's finances recovered somewhat, but he was plagued by trade union problems.

In 1937, he sold his dairy cows and opened a guest ranch, which he named Fuller RanchO. A significant feature of the guest ranch was an irrigation lake, lined with willows and other trees, nearly a half mile long and about five hundred feet wide. Guests were encouraged to use the lake for boating, motorboating and fishing.

During the first part of the guest ranch era, O.R. Fuller used some of the ranch land as a poultry farm, located between the lake and the river. The lake, turkey farm and house all appear in 1936 aerial photographs. A 1935 Corona newspaper article states that the ranch boasted fourteen thousand turkeys, twelve thousand chickens and 625 cows and was the largest irrigated farm in Riverside County.

A chapter titled "Eastvale—The Fuller Ranch" in Stanley Reynolds and Fred Eldridge's 1986 publication, *Corona California Commentaries*, quotes a long letter by Marcellie, preceded by an introduction that was probably written by Fred:

> *Most of the farmers worked modest farms, with the exception of the Fuller Rancho, which at its peak contained about 5,000 acres, most of which bordered the Santa Ana River on the north side. Its history was unique in that area. Mrs. Marcellie F. Thompson was the granddaughter of Charles*

> *Henry Fuller, the first Fuller to be in charge of the rancho. Mrs. Thompson wrote that her grandfather pioneered the Pioneer Transfer Company, a trucking and transportation company in the late 1800s. Her grandfather and his brothers came west from Iowa to settle in Southern California. "My grandparents had one son, Olive Ransome Fuller. He was always known by his initials, O.R.," she said.*

The remainder of the Fuller Ranch story in *Corona California Commentaries* is quoted here from Marcellie's letter:

> *My grandfather was Charles Henry Fuller who founded the Pioneer Transfer Co. in Los Angeles in the late 1800s. My grandfather and his brothers came West from Iowa to settle in Southern California. My grandparents had one son, Olive Ransome Fuller. He was always known by his initials O.R. When my grandfather came West, he and Grandmother divorced. In 1898 when my father was 18 he came to California and worked with his father for a time before going into business for himself. I do not know the exact time, or from whom the ranch was purchased, but about the time of the end of World War I my grandfather bought the ranch in Corona.* [It had been owned jointly by various Fuller family members since about 1889. Marcellie's statement, that Charles Fuller bought the ranch near the end of World War I, probably refers to Charles obtaining sole ownership, or at least a controlling interest, when his younger brother Ortus died in 1922.]
>
> *Grandfather was in ailing health in the 1920s, and my father, O.R. Fuller, bought the ranch in 1925 or 1926. My father also purchased additional acreage in the area to bring the total to 3,000 acres. In later years he leased the river bottom from the government, which is why you heard the ranch was 5,000 acres. He named the ranch Fuller RanchO. (RanchO, with capitals at each end, was the way he had it on all letterheads.)*
>
> *My father O.R. and my mother Ione had the home now occupied by a boys home built in 1928. They named their home Casa Orone, combining their names. A cabinet-maker from Italy hand-carved all the beams and balconies. The original rugs, and most of the furnishings, were imported from Spain. Until 1932, we only were on the ranch weekends and vacations. We lived in Hollywood. At the ranch, a manager saw to raising crops and running the dairy.*
>
> *My father had several dealerships for Auburn, Cord and Duesenberg automobiles in Southern California. During World War I he had a*

dealership in Los Angeles for White trucks. After that he founded what was Motor Transit Bus Company throughout [Southern] *California. In 1928 he sold out to Greyhound for three million dollars which was a heap of money in those days.*

In 1932 when the depression really hit, Dad lost a fortune in the automobile business. It was then we moved to Corona [known by its post office address, actually in present-day Eastvale]. *It was a struggle to hold on to the ranch, but Dad was a very determined man. He worked hard at making a go of ranching. He built up dairy home-delivery routes in Pomona, Ontario, and San Bernardino which he sold to Knudsen about 1940. In 1939 and 1940 he raised 100,000 turkeys which he marketed.*

The guest ranch known as Fuller RanchO Guest Ranch was opened in June 1937. During World War II it was a popular meting place for many of the doctors, nurses, and patients from the Naval Hospital in Norco.

I worked as a hostess from June 1938 to June 1939, when I married. [Marcellie and Clifton Powers moved to another house on the ranch.] *During this time, a movie was made on the grounds and on the lake. During this same period, the ranch was popular with Hollywood celebrities. Many of them were most interesting to know. Those spending time with us were W.C. Fields, Jack Oakie, Groucho Marx, Red Skelton, Spencer Tracy, Mary Pickford and Buddy Rogers, Jeanette McDonald and Gene Raymond, Rochelle Hudson, Claire Trevor, Ken Murray, and writer Garson Kanin.*

In 1938, Dad decided to sell view lots along a lake front [facing the Santa Ana River]. *The first was sold to actor Charley Grapewin. When Mrs. Grapewin died, Charley sold his home to a Dr. Schnack from Honolulu, Hawaii.*

Other lots were sold to a talent scout from Hollywood, a film director, an oilman from Long Beach, a shipbuilder from Long Beach, and a mortician from Long Beach.

Dad died at home of cancer in August 1946. Although Mother was in poor health, she kept the place open to the public through December of 1947. After my father's death I built a home on Grapewin Avenue, which I sold in the late 1950s to Mr. and Mrs. W.A. Cropper.

Mother died, also of cancer, in August 1951. To settle my mother's estate, the family home and the remaining acreage had to be sold. The buyer was a dairyman, Mr. Koenig, who purchased it in 1954.

There were many happy times at the ranch, and many sad times too. It makes me sad to think about the ranch being in the Fuller family for so

> *many years, and now it has been sold to people who can never have the feeling for the place that was home to me for so many years.*

Marcellie lived on the ranch from 1931 until after 1951. She married Clifton Powers in 1939 and Arthur Thompson about 1948.

Part of Fuller Ranch was sold in 1959 to Good Samaritan Centers as a retirement center for the Lutheran Church. From 1967 until at least 1997, the buildings were occupied by St. Katherine's Home for Boys, a residential counseling center for troubled teens overseen by Greek Orthodox clergy. The entire complex was demolished in 2004 to accommodate a residential development.

Chapter 4

EASTVALE ELEMENTARY SCHOOL

Eastvale Elementary School District was created, along with Riverside County, in 1893. During the past 120 years, four elementary schools have borne the Eastvale name. Housing for the school during the first 20 years was at Fuller Ranch, near the corner of Chandler and Harrison Avenues. In 1913, as population increased and shifted farther from the river, classes were moved to a new building about two miles north, on Sumner Avenue, that served for 45 years. Then the district was "unified" with Corona and Norco schools, and a third Eastvale School building was constructed on Orange Street, occupied in 1958. After a hiatus when Eastvale elementary students were bussed to Norco, the site on Orange Street was recently reconstructed to become the fourth incarnation of Eastvale Elementary School.

During the early days of Riverside County history, official school records—if there were any—were apparently not preserved. But many Eastvale School District events seem to have been considered newsworthy. Many references appear in newspaper archives from Corona, Riverside and Los Angeles, and this chapter quotes several of these.

4.1 Origin of Eastvale School District

Eastvale School District Is Created with Riverside County

When the year 1893 began, the Santa Ana River Valley eastward (upstream) from present-day Prado was in San Bernardino County. The land was sparsely populated, with a few farms along the north side of the river and Fuller Ranch headquarters on the bluff about two miles east of Cucamonga Creek. On the west bank of the creek was Valley School, which served children of elementary school age living on nearby farms including Fuller Ranch.

On 2 May 1893, the political situation changed dramatically when voters confirmed their desire to detach most of San Bernardino County south of about 34.03 degrees north latitude (divided along a main survey township boundary line, parts of which correspond to present-day Philadelphia Street on the northern edge of Eastvale and Jurupa Valley, six miles south of Mount San Bernardino Base Line). This part of San Bernardino County was connected with a segment of northern San Diego County to form the new county named Riverside.

Already anticipating a favorable vote on the Riverside County proposal, a convention in Riverside on 5 April had nominated a slate of members for the Riverside County Board of Commissioners. Steps were underway to organize the necessary districts and committees for activating the county. One action of these commissioners was to establish fifty-two school districts for the new county.

A segment of land surrounding Chino, south of the 34.03-degree survey line, remained in San Bernardino County. Valley School was in this segment, on present-day Chandler Street, just west of the county boundary and about two miles from Fuller Ranch headquarters. There is no rule prohibiting a school district with portions in more than one county, as exemplified by Union Joint School District at Mira Loma, which included parts of both Riverside and San Bernardino Counties. Thus it would have been legally possible to maintain existing Valley School District boundaries, so that students who found themselves in the new county would not need to disrupt their lives with a sudden move to a new school. But this seemingly logical step was not taken.

There is some speculation that the founding fathers considered that the new school district would provide an *eastern* campus for *Valley* school, and this idea may have suggested the name for *Eastvale.*

County School Superintendent to the Rescue

"Eastvale" is shown on the list of fifty-two elementary school districts created for the new Riverside County. Each of the districts was, of course, expected to educate children who resided within its jurisdiction, presumably beginning right away in the fall of 1893. A clerk's name is shown on the list for forty-eight of the districts, Eastvale being one of the four exceptions. Some further organization seems to have been needed. However, a preliminary census of school-age children in the Eastvale area did not find enough students to satisfy the prescribed minimum attendance requirement.

Dr. Lyman Gregory, superintendent of schools for the new Riverside County, decided to take matters into his own hands. He set out for Eastvale to get the district organized, to have the school census retaken and to appoint school district personnel. The *Riverside Daily Press* contains several reports of his activities during the first two weeks of September 1893, demonstrating that he spent much of his time during that period at Eastvale.

To the delight and gratitude of Eastvale district residents, Dr. Gregory succeeded. He retook the census himself, finding the eleven children previously counted and eighteen more children who could attend the school.

The Eastvale school board hired Miss Grace Fuller, a younger sister of ranch owners Ortus and Charles Fuller, as the first teacher at the elementary school, and classes began on Monday, 11 September 1893. Records show that Miss Fuller taught at Eastvale for two years, with as many as twenty-nine children in eight grades.

Eastvale School District Gets Underway

Beginning in fall 1893, until a new Eastvale schoolhouse could be built, classes were held at a temporary site, the precise location of which is not known. But there are reasons to believe that it was on Fuller Ranch—the only place where one might have expected to find classroom space. Ortus Fuller was on the board, and his daughters—Rhea, born in 1892, and Muriel in 1895—would later be eligible to attend.

At the end of 1893, it was reported that Eastvale had been allocated $129.28 from the County School Fund. It was the smallest apportionment given any school in the newly formed county, reflecting the fact that Eastvale was the smallest school in the county. When further money was received from the state in January 1894, Eastvale was given another $220.00, again the smallest amount given, but at this time, there were two other schools in the county that received the same amount.

In March 1894, during the spring of the new county's first school year, a Riverside newspaper mentioned Eastvale among a handful of districts in Riverside County that were planning bond elections to raise money for schoolhouse construction.

On 2 June 1894, reports of the general election list an "Eastvale schoolhouse," wherever its temporary site may have been, as a polling place for the Rincon precinct.

In September 1894, Eastvale school trustees asked the County Board of Supervisors to approve a special tax levy of $300. This was presumably for school supplies or fixtures of some sort. The Board of Supervisors approved the special levy.

In November 1895, Eastvale district finally held a bond election. The County Board of Supervisors, at its 6 November 1895 meeting, approved results of the election and issuance of $2,500 in bonds for the school district. The bonds were sold in January 1896.

A school census in May 1896 reported that Eastvale District had thirty-six children between the ages of five and seventeen. School attendance was growing! Of the fifty-two school districts in the county, at least thirty-one had fewer students than Eastvale.

On 18 May 1896, the *Riverside Daily Press* reported that a well had been bored and that the district had contracted with Ed Bloom of South Riverside (as Corona was still called) to construct the schoolhouse for $1,558.

First Eastvale Schoolhouse on Fuller Ranch

Riverside County archives include a deed dated 22 August 1896, when schoolhouse construction was already nearly complete, transferring land from Charles H. and Nellie Fuller to Eastvale School District, for a token price of ten dollars. The deed stipulates that the land is to be used only for school purposes, and title reverts to the original owner "in case such premises and appurtenances cease to be used for such purposes." The 150- by 350-foot lot (about 1.2 acres) was located at "the Northwest corner of the Northeast quarter of Section 2 in Township 3 south of Range 7 West," which is adjacent to later Fuller Ranch headquarters buildings, at the southeast corner of the intersection of present-day Chandler Street and Harrison Avenue.

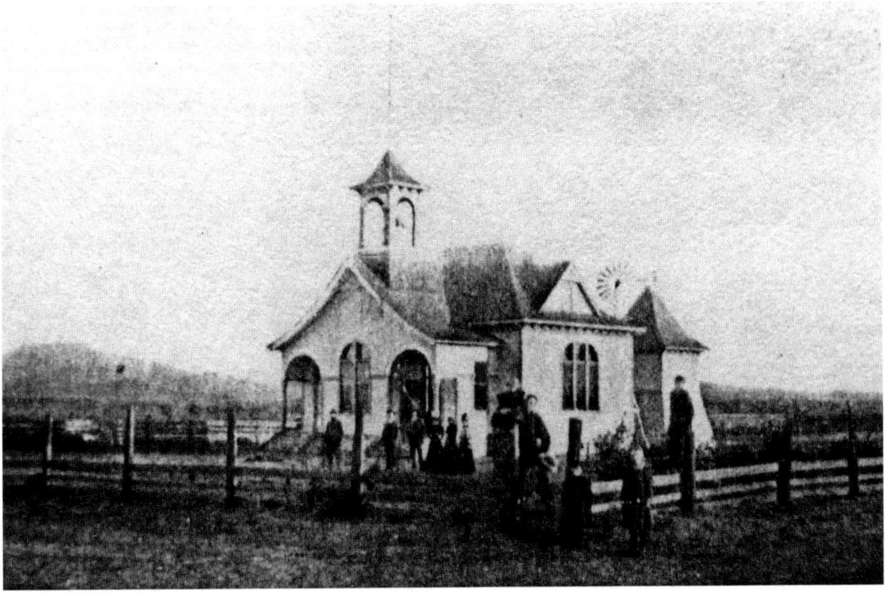

A one-room Eastvale schoolhouse was constructed at the southeast corner of present-day Chandler Street and Harrison Avenue soon after the district was created. It was in use from fall 1896 until spring 1913. *Courtesy Riverside Public Library, Local History Collection.*

Report of Visit from Riverside Enterprise

The new schoolhouse was built quickly and was ready for the students and their teacher in the 1896 fall term. Eastvale School was featured in a lengthy *Riverside Enterprise* article a few months later, on 24 December 1896:

> *An* Enterprise *scribe paid a visit to the new school house in the Eastvale School District yesterday. The building was designed by Ed Bloom, one of Corona's leading contractors, and could hardly be more suitably arranged, the matter of light and ventilation, two essential things in school construction, not being overlooked.*
>
> *The school is in charge of Miss Zella E. Wood, a young lady of unusual ability and educational attainments. The average attendance is 20. The following grades are taught: first, second, fourth, fifth, and eighth.*
>
> *Miss Wood takes great pride in her primary class which has made rapid progress under her tuition. These tots are experts in advanced kindergarten work. The writer was very much interested in the work of these little ones. The teacher called these midgets to the recitation bench, and drew for them on the blackboard some geometrical figures. As fast as they could be traced*

in chalk the little ones named them correctly. Their instructor then took from a box the different geometrical figures and put the class through an object lesson. The answers were given promptly and correctly. The little ones were then sent to their seats and a box of toothpicks was given them out of which they made triangles, rectangles, etc.

The members of this class spell words of two syllables correctly and thoroughly understand the rudiments of arithmetic and can write the figures and add very well.

Lack of space will not permit of the description of the work of each grade, but it was all done well.

This school is unusually well equipped with first-class seats, maps, globes, and all other necessary paraphernalia, $500 having been invested in the fixtures.

The Eastvale school board were exceedingly fortunate in securing the services of so competent an instructor as Miss Woods has proved herself to be.

On 11 February 1897, the *Daily Press* expressed admiration for the beautiful new Eastvale schoolhouse. That same month, plans were made to celebrate Arbor Day by having the community turn out to help grade the school site, plant trees and shrubs and construct an auxiliary building where the students could eat their lunches. The new lunch building was planned with lockers for each student. Local residents also planned to use the newly landscaped grounds for community picnics.

In the 1898 newspaper photo of "Eastvale School House, Six Miles West of Corona," there seem to be a fairly large number of adults near the building. This suggests that the photo might have been taken during the Arbor Day work party in 1897.

4.2 Moves Toward a Two-Room Schoolhouse

New Residents Want a Closer School

The year 1906 ushered in a period of about six years when residents of Eastvale were discontent with their school situation.

The *Riverside Daily Press* of 30 January 1906 reported:

A petition for the formation of a new school district to be known as the Sunflower district, and to be formed out of a portion of the Eastvale school

> *district, has been received by* [County School] *Superintendent Hyatt. The signatures to the petition represent the parents and guardians of over 22 school census children who reside more than a mile from the public schoolhouse. It will be presented to the Board of Supervisors next week. Their district is in the new alfalfa settlement north of Corona, which has been developing within the last year or so and in which numerous Riverside citizens are interested.* [See Chapter 5.]

The next day, the *Riverside Enterprise* shed a bit more light on the issue of a new district: "New settlers have come into the Eastvale school district in such numbers that they feel justified in starting a new school district. J.J. Jones and twelve other residents of that section have prepared a petition for the new district."

Superintendent Hyatt endorsed the proposal. When the Board of Supervisors met on 7 February 1906, it received the petition for the new Sunflower District but did not act on it. At its 22 February meeting, the board considered another version of the proposal to divide the district, as described in the *Daily Press*: "To secure an additional apportionment of $550 with which to hire an additional teacher and have the benefits of free transportation for students living two or more miles from the school, were the objective of the division." The supervisors never approved the division.

The Sunflower proposal died, but discontent remained. Four and a half years later, in October 1910, the *Riverside Enterprise* reported a visit of County School Superintendent Raymond Cree to Eastvale School District. He found the people agitating the question of forming a new school district. "Most of the children attending the Eastvale school live in the north end of the district, some of them traveling five miles to reach the school. The north end residents, together with those living across the line in San Bernardino county, hope to organize a joint union school district [extending across the county boundary], in which event the attendance in the Eastvale school will be much reduced."

Several factors were at work.

New farms on the tableland farther north were no longer dependent on proximity to the Santa Ana River or Cucamonga Creek, since heavy-duty pumps now available permitted reliance on well water for irrigation. Northward population shift had resulted.

The student load at the existing school was becoming intolerable, as everyone could see. School enrollment numbers indicate an enrollment surge during school years 1905–07.

Ortus Fuller and his brother Charles had moved away from Eastvale before 1901, leaving ranch administration in the hands of a resident manager (see Chapter 3). Thus the active support they had provided for the school district in its early days was no longer present.

And perhaps it was becoming harder to find a teacher who could manage eight grades in a single classroom.

Eastvale Elementary School Enrollments, 1899–1915

Enrollments at Eastvale during many of its first twenty-five years are on record. From 1899 to 1904, attendance averaged twenty-three students, with little variation. Years 1905 and 1907 recorded forty and thirty-nine (1906 data is not available); this enrollment anomaly may be related to a population surge near Cloverdale Road at the time of the Sunflower District proposal. The population in 1908 settled back to twenty-one and then gradually increased to forty-eight in 1915, which is the last year found.

Eastvale Elementary School Teachers, 1893–1913

The first teacher for Eastvale Elementary School District was Miss Grace Fuller, a younger sister of Fuller Ranch owners Charles and Ortus Fuller. Grace taught for two years beginning in fall 1893. She was followed by Miss Sadie Walkem in 1895.

At the one-room Eastvale School near Fuller Ranch headquarters, occupied in fall 1896, early teachers were Miss Zella E. Woods (1896 and 1897), Miss Ruby Hodge (1898 and 1899), Miss Georgia Seger (1900), Miss Florence Easton (1901) and Miss Martha V. Shanklin (1902).

Miss Stella Darling taught from fall 1903 until March 1906. Miss Martha J. Morris, appointed in March 1906, continued through spring 1908.

Miss Ora Hooker was teacher for one year beginning fall 1908. Mrs. Martha King (formerly Miss Martha Morris) returned in fall 1909, continuing the following year until December 1910, when she resigned on account of sickness and was replaced by Miss Ethyl Flynn, who continued through spring 1911.

Gertrude E. Hulse taught in 1911–12, and Pearl G. Ogden followed in 1912–13.

Second Eastvale Schoolhouse, on Sumner Avenue 1913–1958

In the spring of 1912, County School Superintendent Cree held a lengthy meeting with the Eastvale board, a little more than a year and a half after his previously reported visit, to discuss construction of a modern two-room school. Apparently, the board had recently held a meeting with the citizens of the district, at which the public had made it clear that they wanted to sell the current schoolhouse and construct a new one farther north, closer to the center of the Eastvale District and closer to the children who lived in newly developing areas. Very soon afterward, on 25 March, an election approved $10,000 in bonds to purchase a new school site and to construct and furnish a new school building.

In September 1912, the Eastvale board of trustees met in Riverside with three architects to discuss the design of the second Eastvale schoolhouse. Maps and a deed at Riverside County Archives in Moreno Valley describe the four-acre site, on the west side of Sumner Avenue just north of the present intersection with Schleisman Road, which was purchased in November 1912 from James P. and Barbara S. Mushrush. A contract for construction of the new schoolhouse was signed the following month.

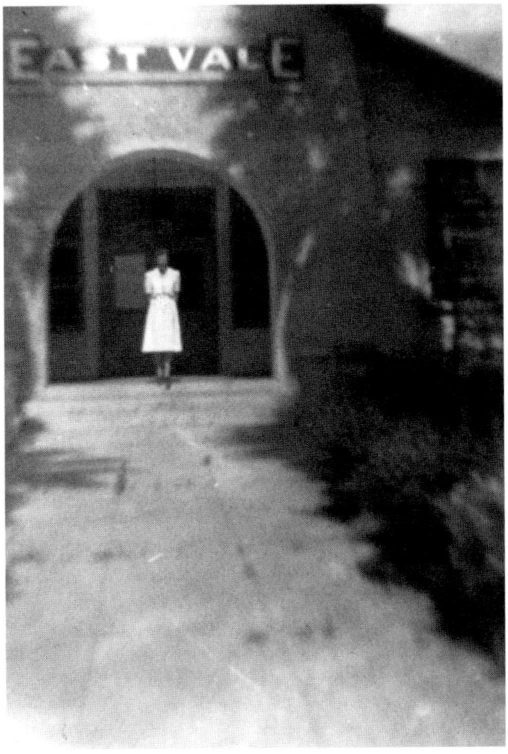

Grace Bynum, shown here, was principal and taught grades five through eight at the second Eastvale schoolhouse, on Sumner Avenue, from about 1937 until 1942. *Courtesy Doris Meissner Klock.*

Also in December 1912, the board sold the previous school building on the Fuller Ranch site to Corona architect and building contractor Leo Kroonen for $7,500. Kroonen also was awarded the contract to build the new school for $7,750. This two-room school would serve Eastvale students for forty-five years, from fall 1913 until 1958.

In 1921, a new state law required all elementary school districts to be annexed to a high school district not more

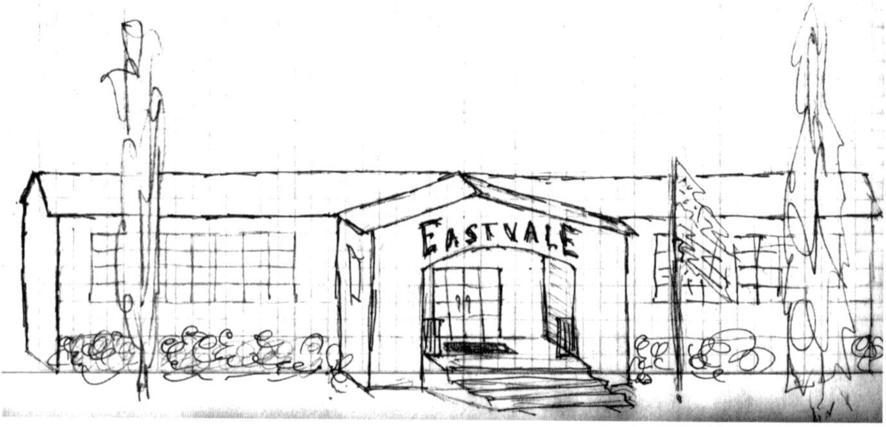

The schoolhouse on Sumner Avenue was occupied from fall 1913 until spring 1958. Sketch from memory by Loren Meissner, 2012.

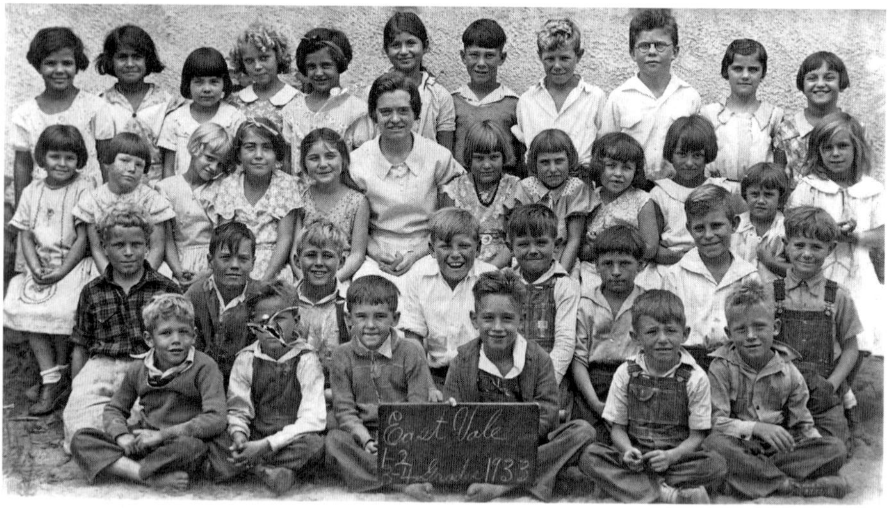

Eastvale photo, 1933, grades 1–4. Loren Meissner's sister Doris (third row, second from left) was in first grade. The teacher was Coreen Gage, who lived with her parents at a nearby farm on Sumner Avenue. *Courtesy Doris Meissner Klock.*

than ten miles distant. Eastvale was annexed in August 1921 to the Corona High School District. Students from Eastvale had already been attending Corona secondary schools, but now the connection was formalized.

Loren attended school at the Sumner Avenue site from 1934 until 1941. He recalls that the two classrooms were about thirty feet square, with a cloakroom next to each. On the side toward Sumner Avenue were two small rooms: a kitchen with a sink, and a lounge with a cot where a sick child could rest until taken home. Between the classrooms was a room called the library, which was used mostly as a storeroom until the population boom after World War II, when it was converted to a third classroom. In front of the library was an open reception area used during public events at the school. At the rear of the school was a blacktop playground with a rudimentary baseball diamond, swings and a few other recreational facilities.

4.3 LATER YEARS

Riverdale Acres: More Pupils—Busing

A major change to the character of Eastvale School District occurred after 1925. A subdivision called Riverdale Acres with about five hundred one-acre lots was created in that year, south of the present alignment of Limonite Avenue, toward the Santa Ana River flood plain east of Wineville Avenue. This was not a "development" in the modern sense, with mass-produced houses constructed for sale. Residents purchased bare lots where they could build a house and raise a few animals, fruit trees or vegetable crops.

The Limonite alignment had been established much earlier as a boundary between political townships and between elementary school districts. Riverdale Acres was in Temescal Township and in Eastvale Elementary School District, although it is outside the boundaries of the present-day city of Eastvale.

The student count at the two-room Eastvale schoolhouse on Sumner Avenue gradually grew as the Riverdale Acres population increased. But the school capacity anticipated in Kroonen's 1912 design proved adequate to accommodate the additional load for many more years.

The most noticeable effect on Eastvale District affairs was the need for bus transportation from the Riverdale Acres subdivision, which was more than two miles east of the elementary school. Busing was provided not only for elementary students from Riverdale Acres but also for farm families along Cloverdale (present-day Limonite) and Archibald Avenues. The bus also scheduled trips for secondary school students from north of the river to Corona Junior High and High Schools.

Corona Junior High School served grades seven, eight and nine, but Eastvale Elementary School maintained seventh and eighth grade classes.

This arrangement required an awkward transition between eighth and ninth grades, from the rural school setting with a few students from each of four grades in one room, to an urban school with large classes that changed hourly by subject. But the arrangement probably resulted in lower school taxes for Eastvale residents.

The bus driver during the 1930s was Charlie Jump, who lived at the end of Riverdale Acres farthest from the school. His morning ritual began with a drive westward, along Holmes Avenue, picking up secondary school students for Corona. He crossed over Hamner Avenue and made a loop around Cloverdale Road, Archibald Avenue, Chandler Road and Schleisman Road, after which he continued to Corona over the Hamner Avenue bridge and through Norco. Most years he had a light load, so he got extra money from the Corona School District for picking up specific students along Hamner Avenue as he went past. The bus route continued west around Corona's Grand Boulevard circle to the high school on West Sixth Street and to the junior high school on Main Street at south Grand Boulevard.

Charlie then drove back out across the river on Hamner Avenue and through Riverdale Acres via Holmes Avenue. Most years the bus turned around on Holmes at Charles Avenue. Then the bus returned along Holmes Avenue, stopping every block to pick up a few Eastvale students, and crossed Hamner Avenue to the school (via Schleisman and Orange) to unload. Another sweep went north on Sumner Avenue to Cloverdale Road, south on Archibald Avenue, back eastward on Chandler Road and to Eastvale School picking up the farm-side elementary students. Charlie was free for the day, until afternoon when he repeated the whole ritual in reverse.

A boy called Duke lived on Holmes Avenue in Riverdale Acres and attended Eastvale in the upper grades. As Charlie came back from Corona on Holmes Avenue past Duke's house, toward the beginning of his Eastvale run, he would give a blast on the bus horn that awakened Duke. When the bus got back to Duke's corner about ten minutes later, heading toward Eastvale, Duke came running out of his house with his pants on, his shirt and shoes in his hand and his breakfast toast between his teeth.

During the major Santa Ana River flood in March 1938 (see March 1938 in the timeline in Appendix B), almost all roadways across the river were impassable for a few days, blocking secondary students from access to their schools. Long detours were required on some routes for several weeks. The channel of Day Creek, seasonally dry and no more than a trickle during most winters, descends from the base of Cucamonga Peak and passes through the middle of Riverdale Acres near the intersection of Holmes and Lucretia

Avenues. For a few days in March 1938, this channel flowed deeply enough to hinder automobile passage from one side of Riverdale Acres to the other, until the water subsided.

Eastvale Recorder Band

County superintendents visited rural schools in the county at least once each year, including Eastvale, until 1947 when it became part of Corona (later Corona-Norco) Unified School District. Superintendents were Lyman Gregory (1893–1895), Edward Hyatt (1895–1907), Raymond Cree (1907–1919), Ira C. Landis (1919–1926) and Ezra E. Smith (1926–1951).

Subject matter specialists also visited the outlying schools a few times a year. In the late 1930s, this included physical education specialist Mr. Lunt, music specialist Miss Prouty, art specialist Ms. Hurd and a school nurse who changed from time to time.

Paloma Priscilla Prouty was a true believer in exposing rural schoolchildren to music. She held a cantata at Riverside Municipal Auditorium each spring, where students from all her rural elementary schools sang in unison after rehearsing independently. In 1939, Miss Prouty chose Eastvale for a model recorder band because upper-grade teacher Grace Bynum was an accomplished flute player. Most of the Eastvale upper graders purchased

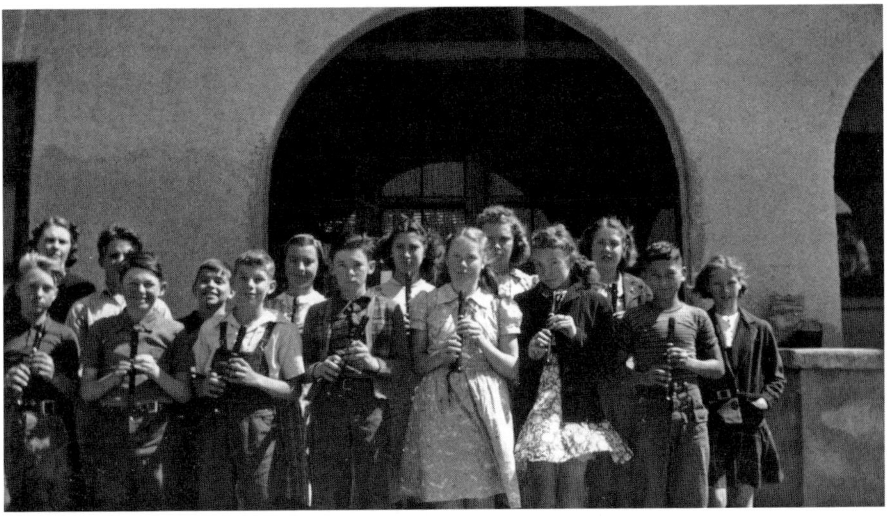

In 1939, a recorder band was organized at Eastvale School. *Courtesy Doris Meissner Klock.*

recorders, mass-produced at about three dollars—a strain on some Depression-era budgets.

After they had attained some degree of proficiency, the budding Eastvale musicians visited other schools—former students recall visiting rural elementary schools near Alvord, Alberhill and Perris. Inspired by these visits, and otherwise by Miss Prouty, some of the other schools also formed recorder bands, and they played in unison as an extra feature of that year's cantata.

Eastvale Farmers Resist School District Unification

Meanwhile, in the older western part of Eastvale, land subdivision retained larger lot sizes required for agriculture. The Fuller Ranch occupied a few thousand acres along the Santa Ana River. Many other Eastvale farms were 80 or 160 acres. Ford-Chase Ranch was originally 640 acres (one square mile), and William Eldridge's portion, known as Premier Ranch, was a little more than 320 acres (one-half square mile). (See Chapter 5.)

Corona school superintendent Frank Bishop reported in 1947 that Eastvale was opposed to joining the Corona Unified School District. Fred Eldridge wrote in *Corona Commentaries*, "The Eastvale School District was made up of farmers and dairymen who looked upon the gathering of the other schools into a 'unified' school district with some suspicion. All Eastvale would get out of it would be the privilege of helping to retire the bonds the others had voted, they figured. So they demanded an Eastvale School District election. Bishop, knowing full well how that election would come out, told his Board that they wouldn't get everybody into unification that year. However, the Riverside County Board of Supervisors, who could count the Eastvale votes, moved the Eastvale District in with the others with no by-your-leave."

At the time of unification, World War II (1941–1945) had just ended and postwar reconstruction was underway. The Great Depression of the 1930s had lowered the U.S. birth rate for economic reasons, and after 1941 most American males of parenthood age were in wartime military duty. The year 1946 is designated by the U.S. Census Bureau as the beginning of the postwar "baby boom," a period of about eighteen years after potential fathers were released from military service.

Eastvale school enrollments were affected by this population surge. An increased number of children were born into families that remained at Eastvale from prewar days and to new families that were forced toward Eastvale from Los Angeles and Orange Counties by similar population pressures there.

The two classrooms at the Sumner Avenue schoolhouse became inadequate. Unused space that had been reserved for a library became a third classroom. Students in the upper grades were transferred in several stages to Corona and Norco. Mildred Fleutsch, who administered Norco and Eastvale elementary school affairs during this difficult period, alleviated the problem somewhat by transferring seventh and eighth grades to junior high school at Corona. Eastvale students in fourth through sixth grades were bussed to Norco, joining Norco residents of like ages at temporary quarters that were released by the navy after the war and, after 1949, at a new schoolhouse at Norco.

A few years later, the Unified District constructed a third Eastvale Elementary School building, with classrooms for six grades, on Orange Street, where classes began in fall 1958.

The Sumner Avenue school was sold in November 1960. Aerial photos of the Sumner site from 1959, soon after classes had moved away, show the building still standing. But later photos from 1967 show a private residence at the former school site. Present-day online satellite maps reveal twenty residences on the four-acre site in Eastvale where Eastvale Elementary School had served elementary students for forty-five years.

By 1982, student population had dipped at Eastvale Elementary School on Orange Street. The site was converted to a Continuation High School (which was later discontinued), and elementary students from north of the river were bussed to Norco.

More recently, as Eastvale became urbanized, elementary schools were added along with residential tracts. A fourth elementary school with the historic Eastvale name, reconstructed at the previous Orange Street site, opened in 2006.

Elementary School Returning to Old Site

A *Riverside Press-Enterprise* report in July 2005 reports construction of the new Eastvale Elementary School at the Orange Street site and reviews history of the Eastvale schools since the 1947 unification:

> *Life is coming full circle on a nine-acre piece of land where a onetime elementary school-turned-continuation high school will become an elementary school once again.*

> *Bulldozers leveled Phoenix Continuation High School last week, preserving only one building for reuse in the new school, Eastvale Elementary, that soon will rise on its site. Even as the demolition progressed on Phoenix, bordered by Orange Street and Cleveland Avenue, construction workers were busy building the early stages of the elementary school that is scheduled to open next July.*
>
> *The school's history dates back a half century. In October 1947, Eastvale became part of the Corona Unified School District. Voters passed a $2.5 million bond measure in 1957 to raise money to build three elementary schools including Eastvale (the third schoolhouse with this name, on Orange Street), according to Bob Brew, spokesman for the Corona-Norco Unified School District.*
>
> *Eastvale Elementary opened in 1958 and served kindergarten through sixth grade through the 1980–81 school year, Brew said. When school resumed in the fall of 1981, the elementary site reopened as Horizon Continuation High School. The district later changed its name to Phoenix.*

A modern state-of-the-art elementary school now occupies this site, again designated by the historic Eastvale name. As of 2013, five elementary schools in the portion of Corona-Norco Unified District north of the Santa Ana River provide modern-day education for students, in the area that was served more than one hundred years earlier by a simple one-room country school.

Chapter 5

DIVERSIFIED FARMING AT EASTVALE

Between 1838 and 1879, most of the land in present-day Riverside County northwest of the Santa Ana River (including Eastvale) was included in a single ranch comprising Bandini's "Jurupa-Stearns Rancho" (see Chapter 1). On the ranch were vineyards; plots of beans and pumpkins; and fields of wheat, corn and barley—but by far, the majority of the acreage was devoted to livestock: mostly cattle, with some horses, sheep and other animals.

By 1900, most of this land, except for the large Fuller Ranch along the north side of the river, had been subdivided into much smaller farms that were purchased by settlers from the eastern United States, Europe and elsewhere. Horses, cows, sheep and other animals were now less important as a source of farm income than fruits, vegetables and grains.

Half a square mile, 320 acres, was considered a large farm. Although most farmers raised some cows, milk was not their principal product. Fred Eldridge, who grew up on Premier Ranch, has pointed out that "except for the sandy area east of Hamner," Eastvale has fertile soil where crops grow well. Sandy soil on the east is ideal for dry-farmed crops, including grape vineyards.

A *History of Southern California* from 1890 describes diversified agriculture in the Chino Creek basin a few miles west of Corona:

> *THE RINCON is the name applied to a tract lying on either side of the Santa Ana River, from ten to twenty miles below Riverside. This is one*

of the best watered and richest farming sections of Southern California. For miles in extent the valley lowland raises yearly immense crops of corn without irrigation, and the semi-moist lands that lie a little higher, extending at the north through the Chino Rancho nearly to Pomona, produce good crops of small grains, as wheat and barley, much of this land also yielding good corn and other crops.

The station and post office of Rincon is on the Santa Ana division of the California Central (Santa Fe) Railway, about twelve miles south of Riverside, and four miles from the Los Angeles County line. There are two daily mails here, a telegraph and express office, hotel, two general stores, etc:

Some farms grew seed grains such as wheat, barley and oats on portions of their land, rotating the crops and leaving some fields idle each year. There were fruit and nut orchards (peaches and apricots, walnuts and pecans) and olives. Most farms had a few beef cattle, sheep or horses.

Alfalfa was a favorite crop because it keeps growing for several years and the same field is harvested several times each year. The farmers fed some of it to animals and sold the rest at retail. Like other legumes, alfalfa enriches the soil by "nitrogen fixation."

This "diversified farming" era continued, with minor variations, into the 1960s.

5.1 Tree Crops Near Eastvale

Citrus, for which much of the Inland Empire became famous after 1880, did not thrive in the Eastvale area. At higher elevations near Riverside or Claremont, occasional sub-freezing nighttime temperatures were alleviated with "smudge pot" orchard heaters and later with wind machines. But these measures were ineffective or too expensive at low elevations nearer the Santa Ana River, where denser cold air settled.

Peach orchards were successful in the dry sandy soil north of Limonite Avenue. Besides commercial crop sales, orchard growers sold household-size quantities to individuals from towns as far away as Los Angeles, who canned and stored them for the winter in one-quart glass Mason jars.

A forty-acre walnut grove is mentioned at the Walters ranch "on the hill beyond [north of] the bridge" in 1907. Premier Ranch had an extensive walnut orchard.

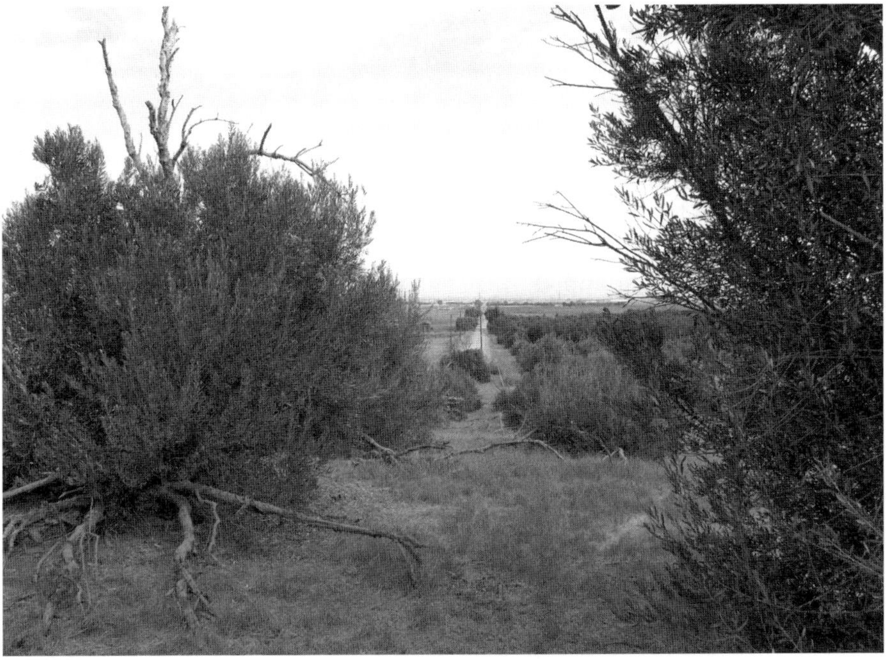

An abandoned olive orchard once owned by Ontario Olive Company, west of McCarty Ranch site, near Cota adobe. Loren Meissner photo, 2012.

An abandoned olive orchard can still be found on the east side of the southward extension of Cucamonga Avenue (west of Hellman) at the edge of Prado Basin, a short distance north of the Bandini-Cota Adobe site. A 1904 map reproduced by Greenwood and Foster shows 110 acres at this location labeled "Ontario Olive Co.," just west of A.R. McCarty's property.

5.2 VITICULTURE—CUCAMONGA VALLEY APPELLATION

Grapes have been an important crop in California for more than two hundred years, according to Eve Iversen:

> *Grapes and the art of wine-making came with the Spanish padres in the late 1700's. Wine-making in the missions was necessary for two reasons: Wine was needed for the celebration of the Roman Catholic mass, and wine was the table beverage of the padres. The grapes grown at the missions probably*

> *had a common origin, which may have been a hybrid of Spanish Vinifera and the wild grapes of California...Mission grapes are but one example of a "heritage crop."*

The first vines in what is now the Cucamonga Valley appellation were planted in 1838 by Tiburcio Tapa, on Rancho Cucamonga, just north of Rancho Jurupa in the Upper Santa Ana River Basin. In 1883, Secondo Guasti (1859–1927) founded the Italian Vineyard Company, which he expanded into a wine enterprise with more than seven square miles of vineyards near the present-day Ontario Airport.

Early vineyards in the Cucamonga-Guasti Wine District were mostly planted with Mission grapes. This variety is now used mainly for fortified wines. Surviving wineries of the Cucamonga Valley appellation produce premium wines, with Zinfandel as a specialty. Cucamonga Valley grape vines are trained to a vertical trunk, rather than a wire trellis.

A website posted by the University of California–Davis mentions early California viticulture developments in Cucamonga Valley. Table grape growers at Etiwanda included George F. Johnston, who was instrumental in developing the Thompson Seedless grape with partner William Thompson. Johnston perfected "girdling"—the removing of a strip of trunk down to the wood of the vine at bloom to increase berry size and set more heavily. Girdling within two to three weeks of ripening can also speed up ripening.

Galleano Historic Winery

The Galleano Winery, still in operation at its traditional site adjacent to the "panhandle" (the northeastern extension) of Eastvale, is one of the few survivors of the sixty wineries that occupied more than fifty square miles of Cucamonga Valley land as recently as 1940. Details can be found at the Galleano website, galleanowinery.com.

Domenico Galleano (1888–1984) and his wife, Lucia (1894–1949), immigrated to the United States in 1913 from northern Italy. In 1927, they purchased the 180-acre Cantu ranch from the family of Colonel Esteban Cantu, a former governor of Baja California.

Domenico's brother John lived nearby with his wife, Madeline (Rossi), and sons Bernardo, fourteen, and John, ten, in present-day Eastvale near Cloverdale Road (now Limonite Avenue), according to the 1930 U.S. Census.

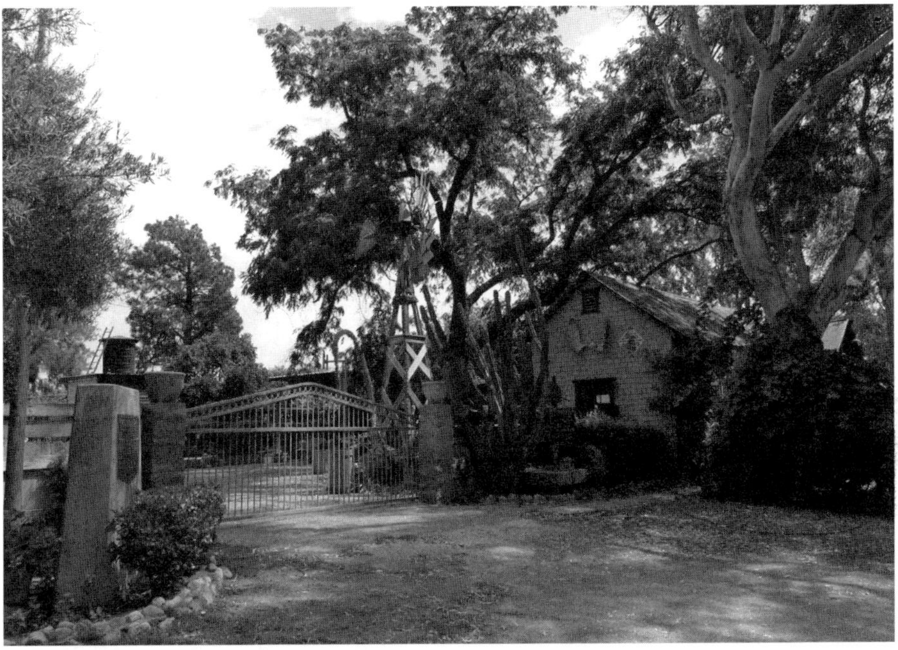

This building once housed the main office at historic Galleano Winery. Loren Meissner photo, 2012. *Courtesy Donald and Charlene Galleano.*

After surviving Prohibition, Galleano vineyards prospered under the direction and hard work of Domenico, his son Bernard (known as Nino, 1914–1983) and his grandson Donald (b. 1952), who is the present owner. It is said that Domenico and Donald were especially competent with regard to growing grapes, while Nino's specialty was winemaking.

In 1939, Domenico Galleano founded the West End Resource Conservation District, establishing a legacy of service by drafting soil conservation policies. In 2005, the district was merged into Inland Empire Resource Conservation District, whose mission is to stop soil erosion and degradation in portions of Riverside and San Bernardino Counties, in cooperation with U.S. Department of Agriculture.

In 2005, the Cantu-Galleano Ranch complex was listed on the National Register of Historic Places. Galleano Winery had previously been recognized as a California State Point of Historical Interest (1992) and as a Riverside County Landmark (1993).

Donald Galleano notes: "There is a great resource of the history of Southern California wine industry at Cal Poly Pomona Library. Contact Danette Cook; you will enjoy it."

Subsurface Tillage

An important contribution to farming methodology emerged from experiences at Galleano Winery. The concept was motivated by conditions found in Cucamonga Creek basin and soon spread to similar low-rainfall farming regions in Canada and throughout the world.

Galleano family patriarch Domenico was attracted to western Riverside County by the sandy soil texture, which permits dry farming and gives the grapes intense flavor characteristics. Dry farming applies to crops with a low moisture requirement (such as grapes) that can survive on natural rainfall with little or no irrigation. Care must be taken to reduce surface evaporation after rain has fallen—but, as a Wikipedia article states, "Some techniques for conserving soil moisture (such as frequent tillage) are at odds with techniques for conserving topsoil."

Specifically, after rainfall, dry farmers often stir up the soil surface with discs or harrows to reduce loss of moisture from capillary action. This technique is used effectively in some parts of Europe but has drawbacks especially in areas of Southern California that are subject to strong northeast Santa Ana winds. In the Cucamonga Valley, meteorological factors favoring a Santa Ana wind often occur a few days after a rain, when topsoil loosened by "techniques for conserving soil moisture" is in ideal position to be blown away.

Domenico Galleano pioneered the technology of subsurface tillage with a wide V-shaped blade that cuts beneath the surface of the ground, slicing the sod roots off underground and leaving mulch on top that acts as a soil protector in heavy wind. Galleano's blade was quickly adopted for wide use in the Cucamonga Valley vineyards but was never patented. Charles Noble from Canada visited Southern California in 1935 and saw a subsurface plow being used to harvest sugar beets. He returned to Canada where he developed the "Noble Blade" and marketed it commercially after 1941.

A recent user describes the effect of this blade on prairie land in Montana: "Then last night (finishing up under a near-full moon) back down again, like a cartoon mole traveling underground, I went over the field with an implement called a Noble blade, which is a 4-foot wide single blade that cuts a few inches underneath the soil, severing the roots of the grass. After making a pass, it hardly looks as though anything happened, but while dragging the implement across the field you can see the grass rising as the blade passes underneath, then falling."

5.3 NORTH FROM CORONA IN 1907

On 12 April 1907, the *Corona Daily Independent* published impressions of an observer on his visit to the Eastvale area. Now, more than one hundred years later, this article titled "Up and Down the Queen Colony" gives us insight into the ranches of that area.

THE DRIVE TO EASTVALE
Until his recent visit the writer had little conception of the great country lying north of Corona. The roads were not extra good, owing to the recent heavy rains, but otherwise the trip was delightful…About four miles north of Corona the road winds to the left of a lofty hill, descending rapidly until it reaches the Santa Ana river.

WALTERS RANCH
On the hill beyond the bridge is the residence of S.A. Walters of Riverside. We found Mr. Walters in the hay field busily at work stacking alfalfa. He gave us facts and figures in a business-like way, and the reporter was able quickly to get hold of the facts concerning the development he saw taking place before his eyes.

Mr. Walters has a ranch of 200 acres, 120 of which is in alfalfa and the balance in grain. A forty of the one hundred and twenty acres is set out in walnut trees, thus making two crops, utilizing the water to irrigate both at the same time. Mr. Walters said it was recommended by scientists to keep a growing crop on the land in the raising of walnut trees, and as alfalfa is rich in nitrogen it acts as a fertilizer for the land as well as nutrient for the trees, giving them life and vigor.

On this ranch a 44-horse power engine has been installed that will raise 150 miner's inches of water. [A "miner's inch" in Southern California is .02 cubic feet per second.] *And this can be done continuously without lowering the water in the well. The water is pure and cold and enhances the value of the property many thousands of dollars. The price at which this ranch is held we understand to be $45,000.*

We would say that while the engine at the water plant is giving perfect satisfaction, emergencies may arise in the future that will require more horse power, and in this event the machinery will be run by electricity, as a wire can be adjusted to the electrical current at Arlington.

The alfalfa on the ranch was looking well, and from what we could learn from observation it is as good as can be found in Riverside county. Mr. Walters expects to cut 1,000 tons of hay from the 120 acres this summer.

One very unique and interesting piece of machinery we noticed on the ranch was a stacker. It has long fingers, and the upper part of it is made on the principle of the buck-rake. Mr. Walters had both in use on the date of our visit. The buck-rake brought up its load and deposited the same gently upon the stacker, and the stacker, being adjusted on pulleys to work up and down, threw its load upon the stack with equal gentleness, thus keeping the leaves on the alfalfa stalks intact, obviating the old method of handling the hay with pitchforks, which method shakes off the leaves and destroys the best part of the hay. This every rancher knows to be true, and as the writer is stating facts he will stand on the wisdom of his own observations.

Ford and Chase Ranch

The Ford and Chase ranch [see Premier Ranch, later in this chapter] *embraces an area of 640 acres, 270 of which is seeded down to alfalfa. The ranch has a pumping plant operated by a 25-horse power engine. The present water supply is inadequate to irrigate the land, and as soon as a well driller can be secured another well will be sunk and another engine installed, which will give ample water supply for the property. The ranch employs about twenty men.*

Grotzinger Ranch

Fred Grotzinger we found at his home breaking bronchos. Mr. Grotzinger has good ranch property and this year has set out one and a half acres of strawberries, the fruit of which will soon be ready for market. Next year he will set out three acres more of the same kind of fruit, which will give the people of Corona all the berries they need fresh from the field.

Visitors are always welcome on the Grotzinger ranch and receive the courtesy and consideration for which California people are noted.

Robert Arborn Ranch

The ranch of Robert Arborn is located in what is known as the Eastvale district [shown on a map just west of Hellman, close to "Valley School 1890" in San Bernardino County; 1910 census lists Arborn residence at Chino], *and consists of 88 acres, 55 being in alfalfa and the balance in pasturage. This ranch is distinguishable from many others on account of free water and plenty of it, the proprietor having purchased the property many years ago and obtained the first right to a large stream running through the land.* [Cucamonga Creek—note: several creeks that flowed into the Santa Ana River in 1907 are now seasonal but may still flow underground.] *This of itself is no small item, especially to those who have to purchase water at a high figure.*

Just below the house a dam has been constructed that holds a volume of water twelve feet deep. This water has been stocked with fish, and many of them will weigh twelve pounds each. In June the fish will be ready for the sportsman and the editor and his staff are cordially invited to be present at that time and participate in the sport of catching them.

The pumping plant is supplied with a 25-horsepower engine, which forces the water to a reservoir or distributing point 525 feet from the plant. Here pipes have been arranged to receive and convey the water to all parts of the ranch. L.C. Kirby farther south, along same creek but on the other side [see adjacent listing on 1910 U.S. Census, Chino] *receives his irrigating water supply from this source also.*

Mr. Arborn is a native of Australia [U.S. census shows England] *and landed in California in 1857. He is the father of twelve children, six girls and six boys, ten of whom are now living. A picture of the family taken some years ago was exhibited at the St Louis Exposition. Mrs. G.S. Branch, a daughter, told the writer that her father and mother were 81 and 82 years of age respectively and if they lived until November efforts would be made to have all the children come home to celebrate their 60th wedding anniversary.*

In 1857 three men owned all the land between San Bernardino and Los Angeles, so it can be readily seen great changes have taken place since that time and as Mr. Arborn and family have resided continuously in what is now San Bernardino and Riverside counties, they can speak authoritatively on everything connected with the growth and development of Southern California for the last fifty years

DEVOE, CHARLES ARBORN, AND BRANCH RANCHES

C.W. Devoe has recently purchased the old Ashcroft ranch of 40 acres and has recently taken possession of the same, but owing to the scarcity of house room in Corona the family who sold the property are still on the ranch, but expect to move soon. The ranch is a nice piece of property and the hay crop is looking well.

Chas. E. Arborn, another ranchman of the same locality [son of Robert, age forty in 1907], *has a ten-acre tract of land on which is a pretty cottage and other improvements in keeping with the up-to-date property around him. The land is sown to barley, and everything in and around the premises denotes thrift and enterprise.*

G.S. Branch was not at home, but his family were there bravely holding the fort and gave us to understand that they were doing well and had no fault to find with California or its environments. They have twenty acres of good hay, a good pumping plant for water, and have every reason to rejoice and feel glad.

Otis Ranch
The F.G. Otis ranch of 307 acres is located on Dale Creek [not found on list of California creeks—possibly should be Day Creek], *and is devoted to hay, pasturage and dairying. There are 92 cows on the ranch, 65 of which are milked, on an average. The cream is separated on the ranch and is then taken to the creamery at Chino.*

The buildings are modern in construction and have been built with a view of stability and convenience. The floors in the barn are concrete, a very desirable feature. Another commendable feature is the arrangement of water mains at each end of the barns for flushing the floors, thus keeping them neat and clean.

The barn accommodates 65 cows, and two men do all the milking, separating, and caring for the calves.

The ranch has two pumping plants, operated by two gasoline engines of 25 and 35-horse power each, and the water being plentiful the ranch never fails to produce good crops.

Mr. Otis is a capitalist and does not live on the ranch himself. He has entrusted his ranch interests to his son, George A. Otis, who has property interests of his own nearby. As George A. cannot look after all the property himself he has engaged Nelson Teeter to manage his father's ranch. Mr. Teeter is a courteous and obliging gentleman, and competent to fill the responsible position he occupies.

5.4 Premier Ranch

Second in influence only to the Fuller Ranch at Eastvale during the first part of the twentieth century was Premier Ranch, which once occupied the square mile of land that has become the heart of Eastvale. Its present-day boundaries are Limonite Avenue, Hamner Avenue, Schleisman Road and Sumner Avenue, the square mile (640 acres) known formally by its survey designation: Section 25 of T2S R6W. As was also the case in early times with other large properties, the

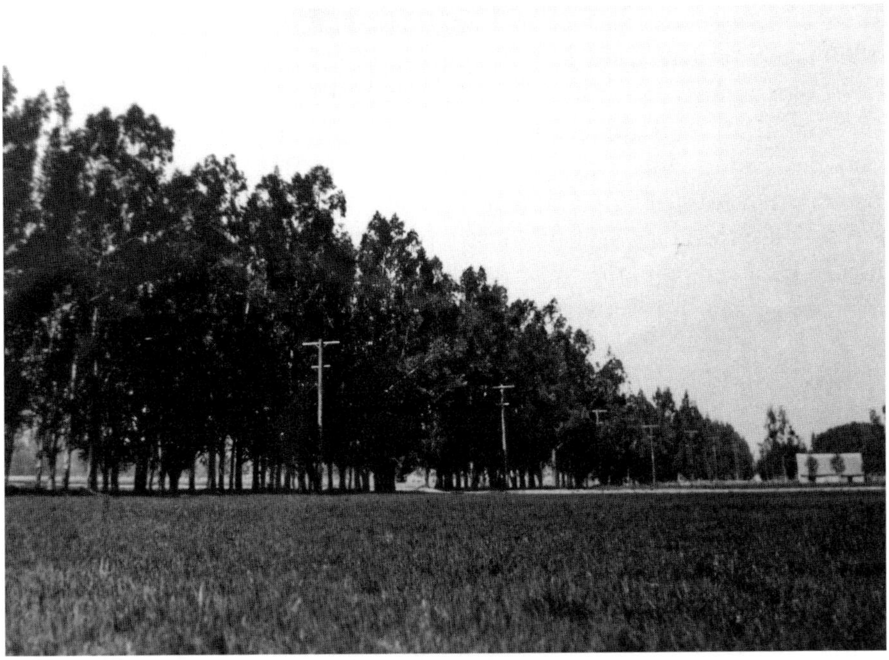

Eucalyptus trees and power poles march alongside a farm field on Premier Ranch. *Courtesy Lynne Eldridge Richie.*

extent of Premier Ranch did not remain fixed—owners purchased adjacent acreage and sold off portions, and by 1909, the largest single segment consisted mainly of the northern half of Section 25, the 320 acres along present-day Limonite Avenue between Hamner and Sumner Avenues.

Other owners of the southern half, extending into the more recent dairy era, are not described in detail here. These included Caleb Harvey and Kurt Iseli.

Early Owners, 1904–1911: Chase and Ford, Schroeter

The ranch first came into prominence in 1904 when it was owned by Joseph Warren Chase and Oscar Ford and was known as the Chase and Ford Ranch. As late as the 1930 U.S. Census, Hamner Avenue was called the Ford-Chase Road.

Joseph Warren Chase, a Civil War veteran born in Ohio in 1829, had moved to California before 1900 and established a dairy and creamery at

Riverside. Oscar Ford, born in Iowa in 1856, listed his occupation in the 1880 census at Riverside as horticulturist. Both men were on the Board of Directors of Riverside County during the county's early years, and Ford served a term as mayor of Riverside beginning in 1914. In a history of San Bernardino and Riverside Counties, James Boyd describes Ford as a nurseryman and fruit grower near Riverside.

Boyd also mentions the venture at Eastvale: "About the year 1904 Mr. Ford turned his attention to the water-development enterprise in the district beyond Wineville, where he secured 770 acres of land, 300 acres of which he planted to alfalfa. Later he disposed of this entire property, upon which he had made excellent improvements, including the development of an effective system of irrigation." New irrigation methods involving wells and pumps were enabling expansion of farmland within California's low rainfall region, beyond areas that could be adequately supplied from river water. Ford was also active in developing distribution of electric power (which soon came to be indispensable for irrigation pumps) and in road construction within Riverside and Orange Counties.

It appears that neither of these early owners of the ranch at Eastvale lived on the ranch. The ranch supported a diversified group of agricultural activities, which was common for that time. A 1907 newspaper article records the size of the Ford and Chase Ranch at that time as "640 acres, 270 of which is seeded down to alfalfa," and describes "a pumping plant operated by a 25-horse power engine. The present water supply is inadequate to irrigate the land, and as soon as a well driller can be secured another well will be sunk and another engine installed, which will give ample water supply for the property. The ranch employs about twenty men."

About 1909, after Chase died, Ford sold 320 acres, the northern half of Section 25, to H.M.E. Schroeter of Long Beach. He was another absentee owner, as explained in an article in the *Riverside Daily Press* on 3 September 1909, which mentioned that O.N. Manlove was the ranch's "efficient foreman." The 1909 article praised the ranch and described its operation: "Of the West Side ranches, the Premier Ranch, formerly owned by J.W. Chase and Oscar Ford of Riverside, is one of the largest and most perfectly developed. There are 320 acres in the property, 240 acres being in alfalfa. Two pumping plants, 40 and 32-horse-power, lift 250 and 175 inches of water, respectively. The wells are 250 feet deep and the water stands within 25 feet of the surface. Sixteen head of work horses and mules are kept busy and 19 men are employed." The earliest known use of the name "Premier Ranch" appears in this article. Mr. Schroeter owned the ranch for two or three years and sold it to William Eldridge in late 1911.

William and Fred Eldridge, 1912–1959

William Franklin Eldridge was born in Illinois in 1878. He attended the University of Chicago, where he played football under pioneering coach Amos Alonzo Stagg on the 1899 championship team. He was awarded his bachelor degree in 1901. Maude Sarah Lee was born in Missouri in 1881 and came to Los Angeles at an early age. In her late teens, she developed an interest in photography and became known as the first female photographer with her own studio in Los Angeles. She later won many prizes for her photos in national competitions.

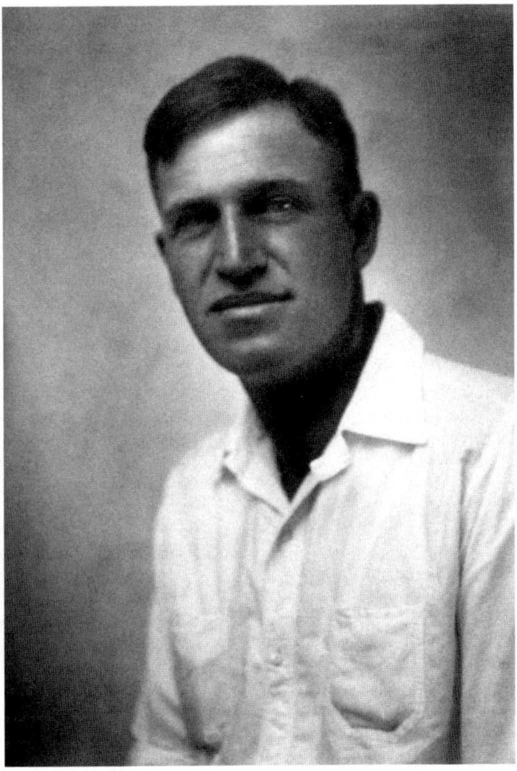

William Franklin Eldridge (1878–1954). *Courtesy Lynne Eldridge Richie.*

William and Maude were married in December 1908 at her family's home in Los Angeles. They moved to Lincoln, Nebraska, where he took "a short course in agriculture" at the university, and then they lived on his father's farm in central Nebraska for a time before returning to California where their only son, Fred, was born in 1911 in Santa Barbara.

In December 1911, William purchased Premier Ranch. The following month the Eldridges moved onto Premier Ranch, where William promptly got rid of a hog operation that had existed. In February, he began advertising the sale of hogs in the Riverside newspapers. One ad declared, "I am going out of the hog business." By 4 March, the ads had changed to state that Eldridge had sold nearly two hundred hogs and had just a few sows and young hogs left for sale at bargain prices.

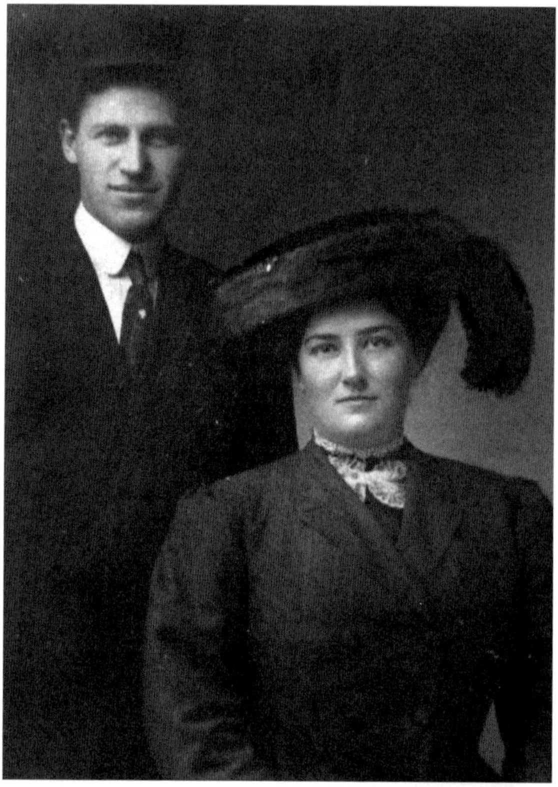

Left: William and Maude Eldridge. *Courtesy Lynne Eldridge Richie.*

Below: William Eldridge, his wife and son lived in this little house on Premier Ranch until they built their much larger adobe home. The silo next to it says "Premier Ranch." *Courtesy Lynne Eldridge Richie.*

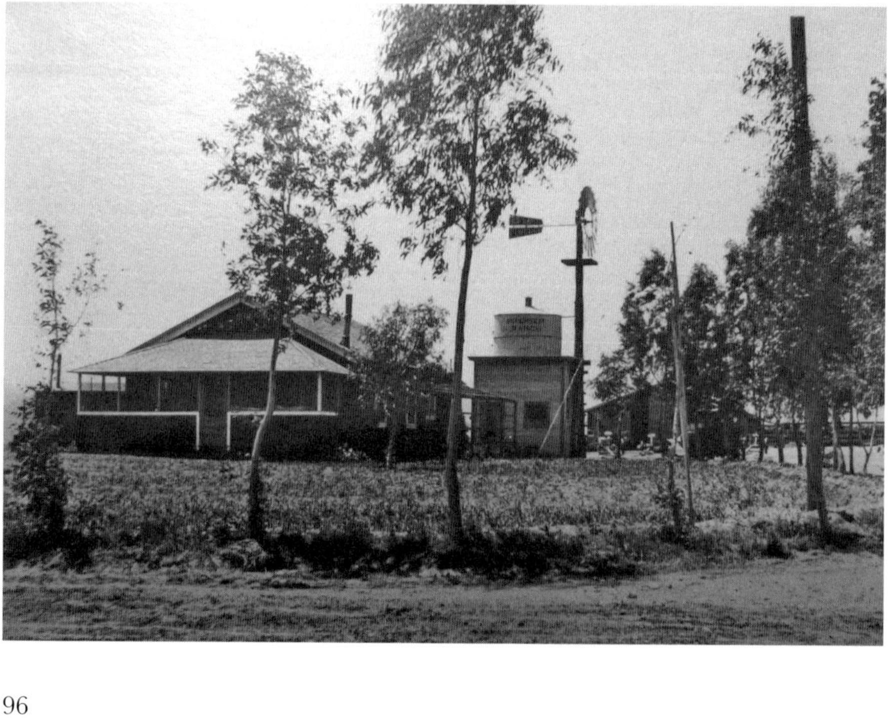

Altogether, Eldridge farmed 361 acres. The 160 or so acres of Payne walnut trees that were a prominent feature of Premier Ranch for many years were probably planted during his ownership. The remaining acreage was devoted to crops such as alfalfa, grain, corn and black-eyed peas.

There was a small house on the ranch that had probably previously housed the on-site manager. The Eldridges lived in that house until they could build a more suitable residence.

William and Maude collaborated on the design of a new ranch house, to be built of adobe bricks made with red clay from the "lower forty" acres of the ranch (a small block of land extending into the south half of T2S R6W).

The new home design was a U-shape with a patio in the middle. Making the home from adobe bricks was a practical decision before air conditioning in the hot summers of inland Southern California. In spite of the new house being made of such a simple material as adobe, the Eldridges created a beautiful, even elegant home for themselves and their son in the rural agricultural district at Eastvale.

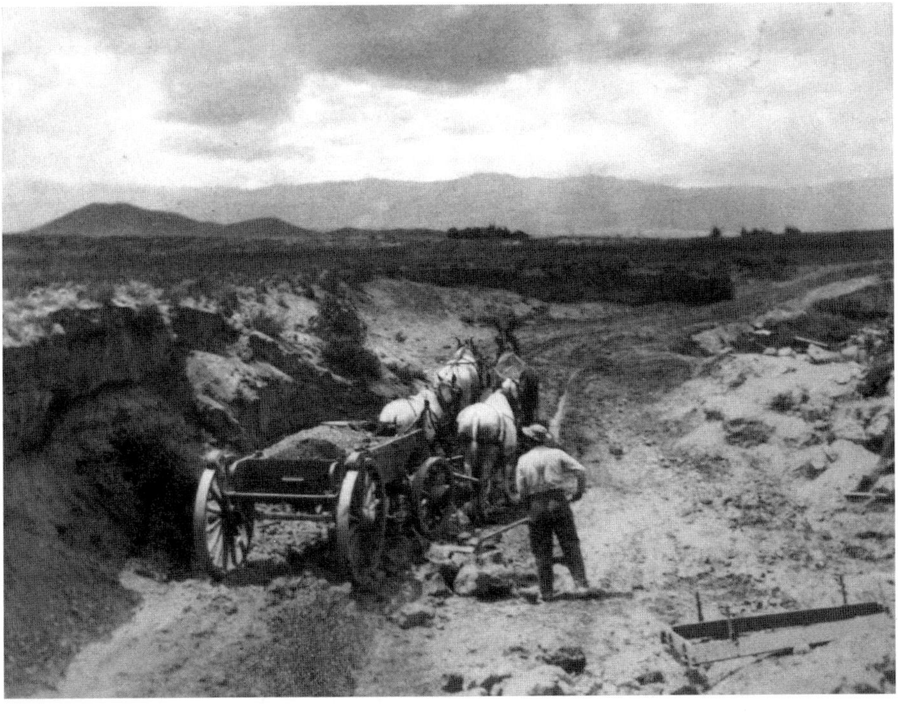

A man piles clay into a wagon to be used to make adobe bricks for the Eldridges' home. *Courtesy Lynne Eldridge Richie.*

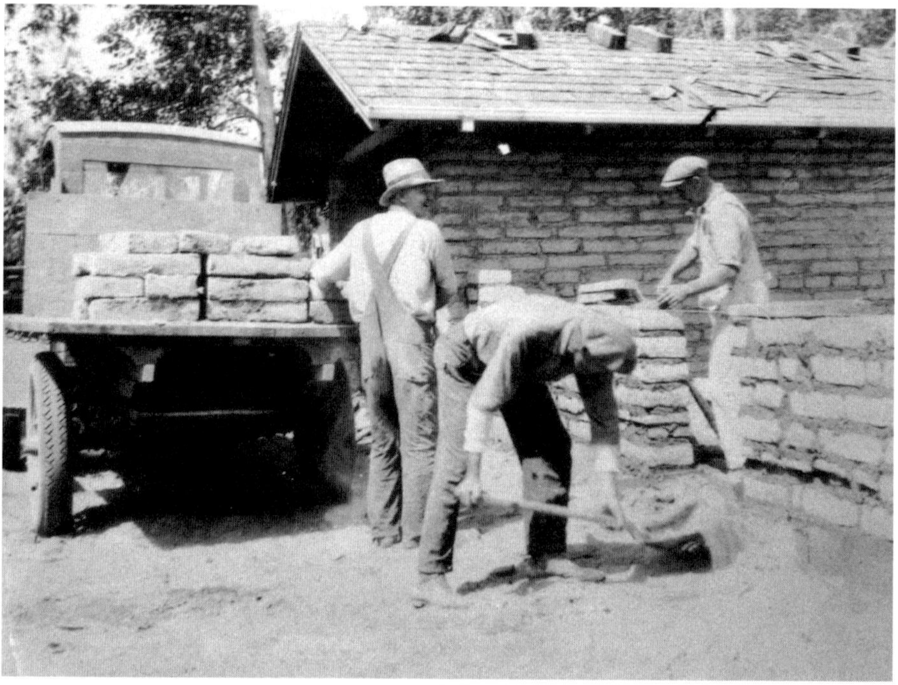

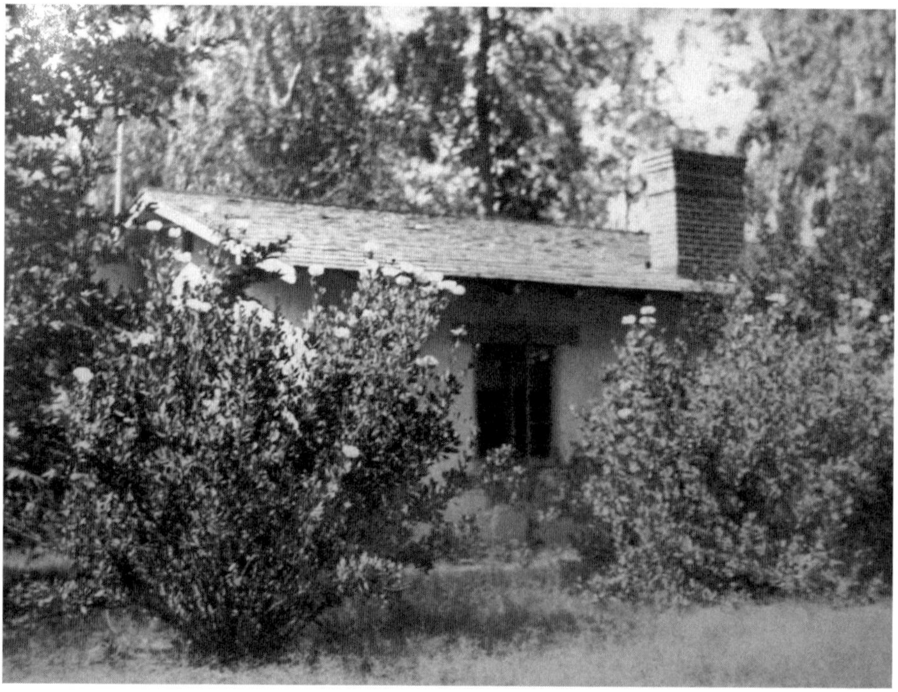

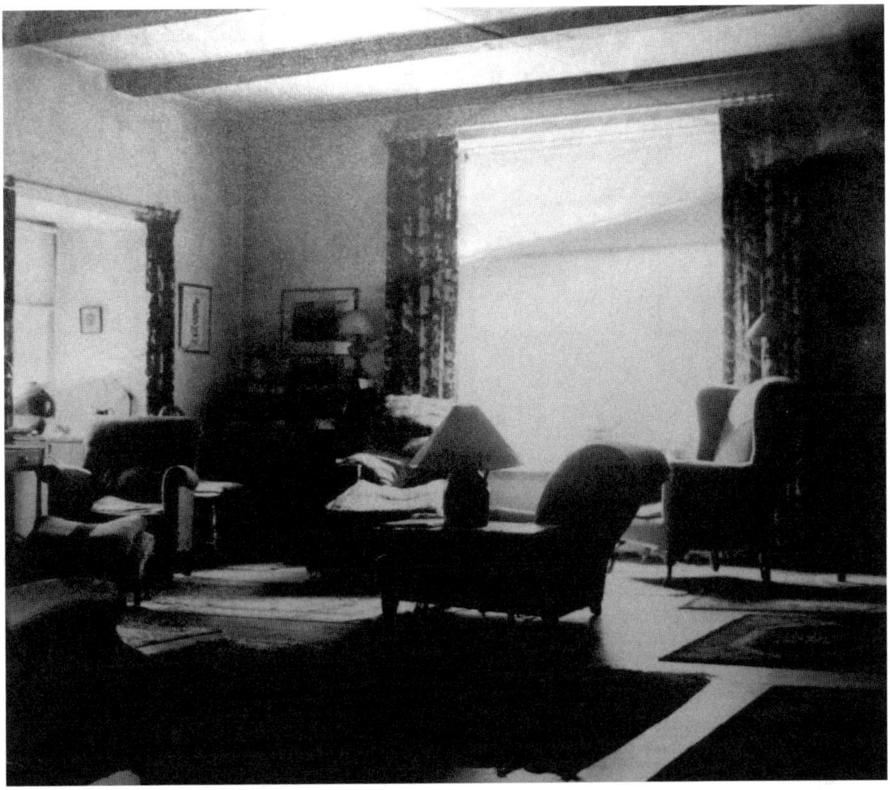

Above: The living room of the Eldridges' adobe home in the 1920s or 1930s. *Courtesy Lynne Eldridge Richie.*

Opposite, top: These men are working on an adobe wall during construction of the Eldridges' home on Premier Ranch. *Courtesy Lynne Eldridge Richie.*

Opposite, bottom: The adobe house built by William Eldridge does not feature in many family photos. This is one of the few in the family photo collection. *Courtesy Lynne Eldridge Richie.*

William Eldridge and his Premier Ranch became well known in Eastvale and throughout western Riverside County. He was influential in various agricultural interest groups. He was a founder and one of the first presidents of the Riverside Farm Bureau, a director for many years of the California Farm Bureau Federation, an officer of the Riverside Production Credit Association, a director of the California Walnut Growers Association and treasurer of the Riverside Walnut Growers Association. During the Great Depression, when the dairy industry collapsed, he organized the Independent

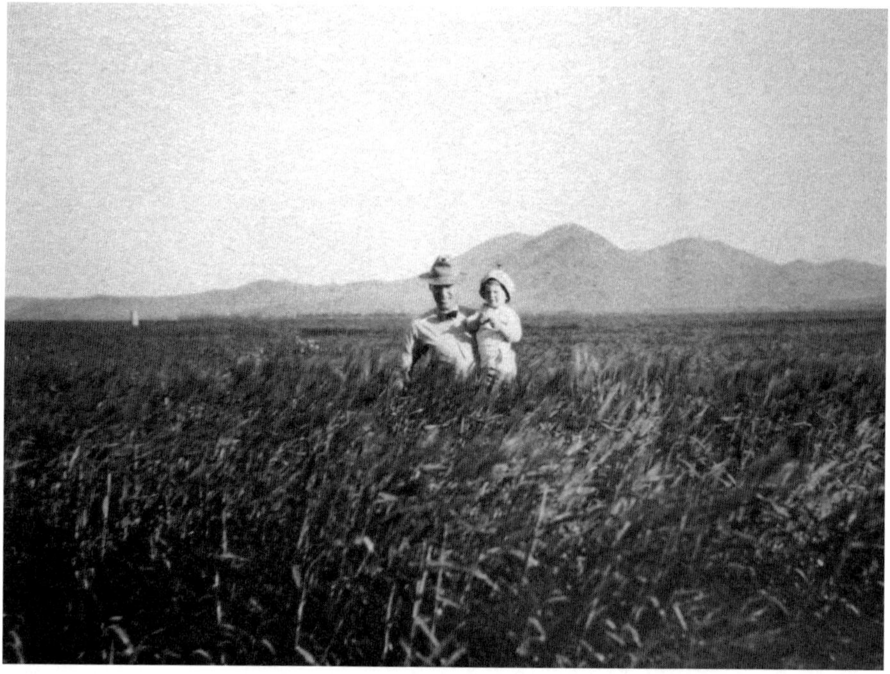

William and Fred Eldridge in a field on Premier Ranch, circa 1912. *Courtesy Lynne Eldridge Richie.*

Milk Producers Association. He became president of that cooperative and was credited with being one of twelve men who were able to get milk control legislation passed to help stabilize the industry.

William Eldridge employed a number of ranch hands on his 360 acres. His dairy operation included as many as one hundred cows that had to be milked by hand twice a day, 365 days a year with no days off. It was a hard life, with constant work and little time for travel or recreation.

The Scamara Family

Swiss immigrant Victor Scamara worked on the ranch for at least thirty years, probably longer than any other employee. Victor was born in 1890 and came to the United States in 1912 at age twenty-two. He was already working for William Eldridge before he married Eleanor Martinez of Chino in 1916. He eventually became the head milker at the dairy.

Victor and Eleanor lived in a small white house on the ranch. There they had six children who lived to adulthood. Margie was born in 1917, Arthur in 1918, Ralph in 1919, Robert in 1921, Victor Jr. in 1926 and Angelina in 1928.

Victor Scamara Jr. is the last surviving sibling of the Scamara family at age eighty-seven (as of 2013). He generously shared memories of his younger days on Premier Ranch. Rather surprisingly, he never remembered hearing the name "Premier Ranch"—it was always just the "Eldridge Place."

Victor Junior remembers that the ranch had a large herd of dairy cattle, raised alfalfa and corn to feed the cows and harvested walnuts from the walnut groves.

The 160 acres of walnut trees were located in four separate groves. The walnuts

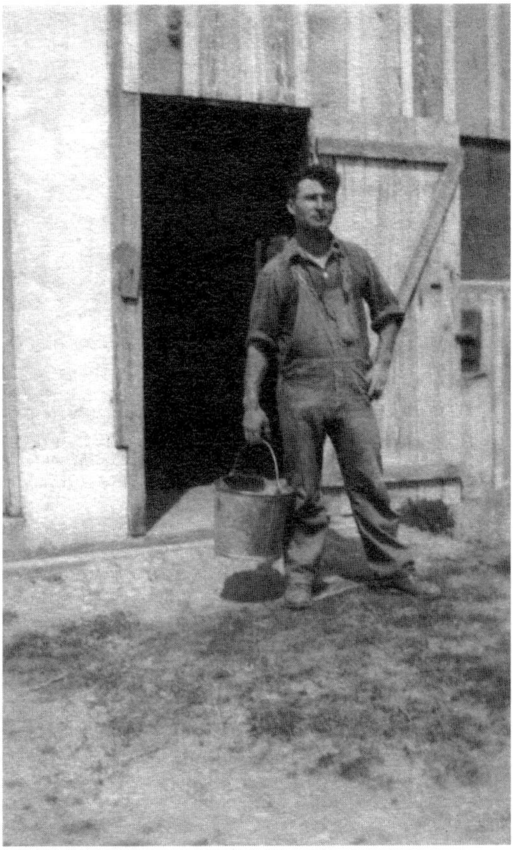

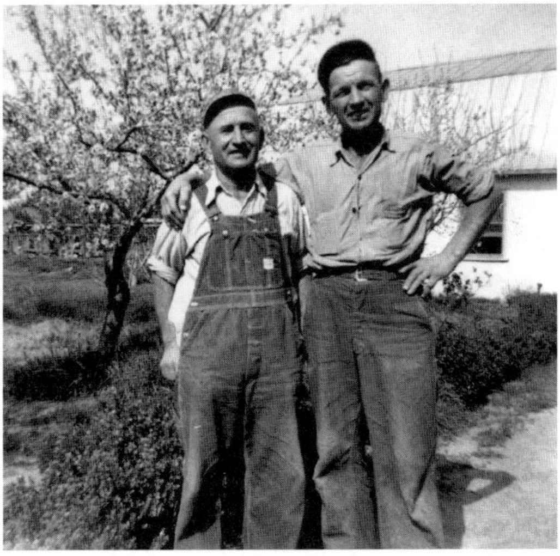

Top: Victor Scamara Sr. stands next to the barn on Premier Ranch holding a milk bucket, circa 1925. *Courtesy Susan Scamara.*

Right: Victor Scamara Sr. (left) with Paul Hostettler on Premier Ranch. Paul and his wife, Pearl, worked and lived for a number of years on the ranch until they moved to Fifty-fourth Street in Mira Loma, where they operated an egg ranch. *Courtesy Susan Scamara.*

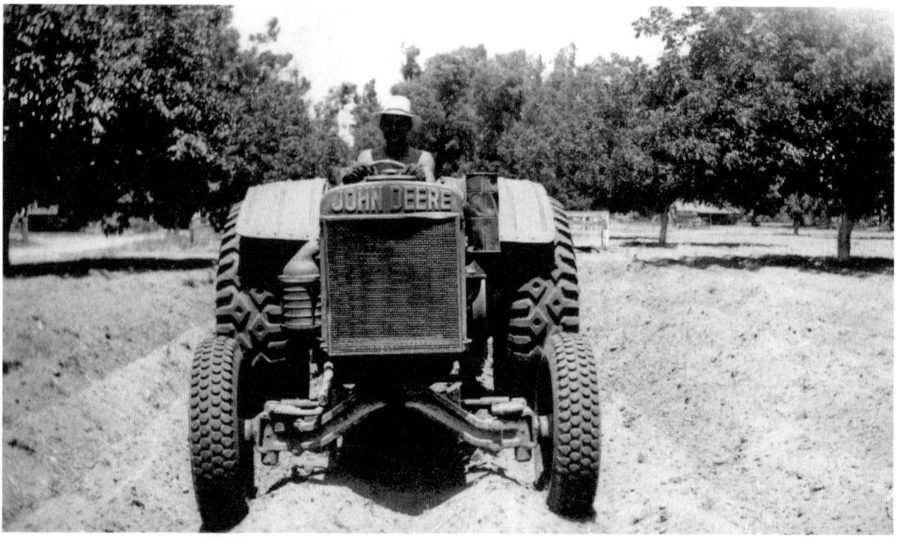
JOHN DEERE

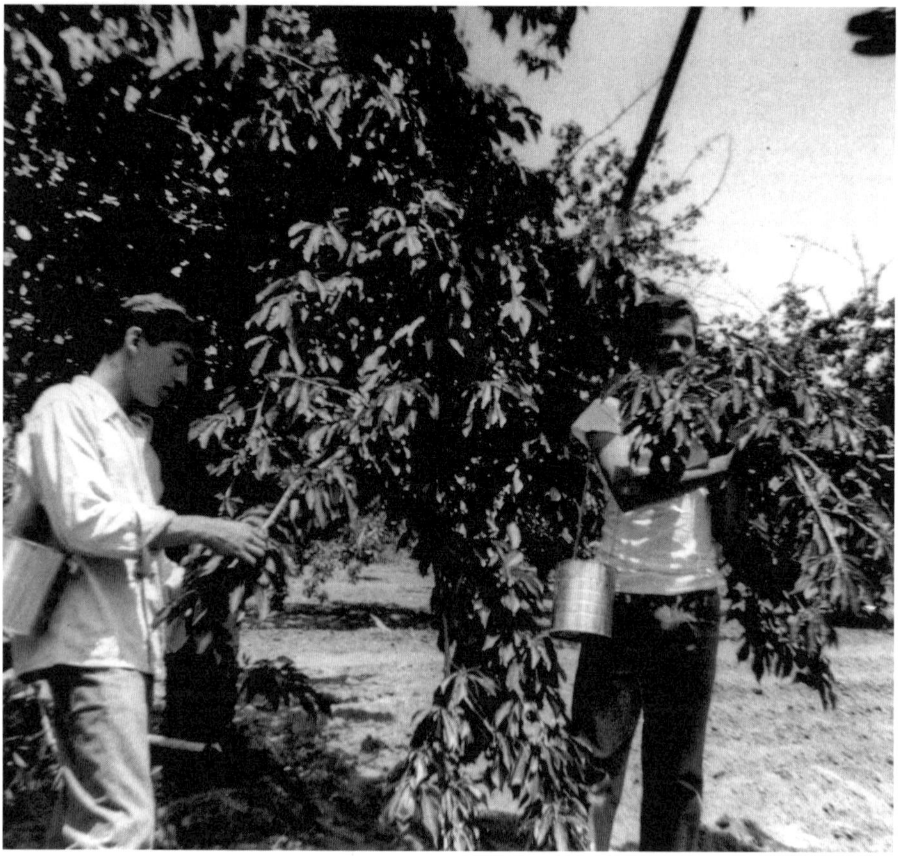

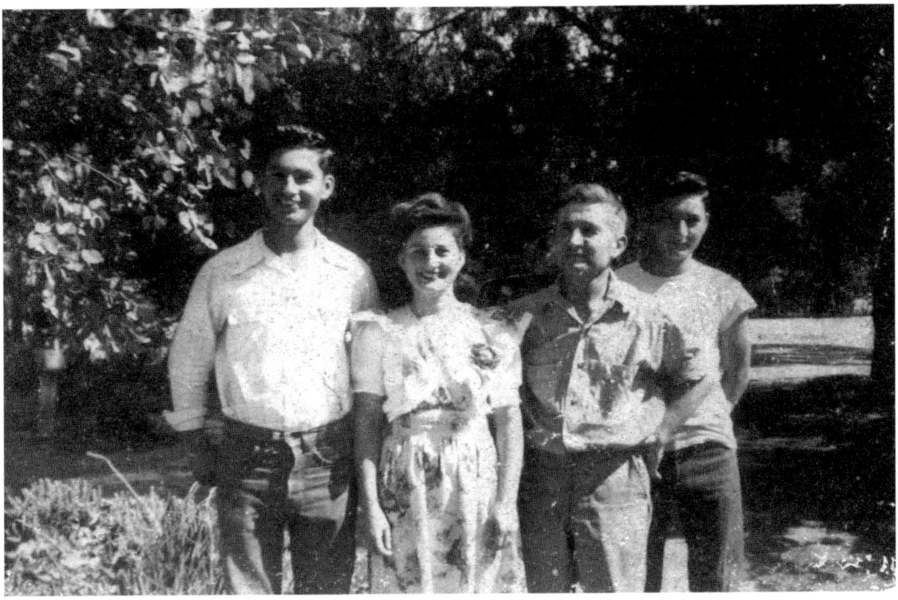

Above: The Scamara family circa 1940s. *From left:* Robert, Marge, Victor Sr. and Victor Jr. *Courtesy Susan Scamara.*

Opposite, top: Victor Scamara Jr. drives a tractor in one of the four walnut groves on Premier Ranch. *Courtesy Susan Scamara.*

Opposite, bottom: Robert Salgado and Lloyd Salgado Jr., grandsons of Victor Scamara Sr., pick walnuts, circa 1953. They wear tin buckets to hold the walnuts. *Courtesy Susan Scamara.*

were harvested in September and October. About ten or twelve pickers who lived near Corona would be hired. They would use long poles with hooks on the end. The pickers would reach that long pole up into the tree, snag a branch and shake it to make the walnuts fall to the ground where they could be picked up. The pickers would also climb up on tall ladders to pick the walnuts. The trees were harvested in this manner twice during the picking season.

The house on the ranch where the Scamara family lived had some walnut trees around it. The Scamara boys began picking the walnuts off those trees when they were ten or twelve. At about the same age, they began to work for "Old Man Eldridge" to earn money for schoolbooks, school clothes and pocket money, although there were few opportunities to spend it in rural Eastvale.

When the boys were older, Eldridge got out of the dairy business and sold off all the cows. However, he allowed Victor and his family to remain in the house on the ranch, probably because the four Scamara sons were still working at the ranch. But after Pearl Harbor (1941), most able-bodied young American men were called into military service. After World War II, Victor Sr. bought a house nearby, on Etiwanda Street in Mira Loma, where he moved after being employed at the Eldridge Place for more than thirty years.

Fred Eldridge

The Eldridges' only son, Frederick Lee Eldridge, was born 29 June 1911 in Santa Barbara, and the family came to Eastvale before he was one year old. He was raised on the ranch and attended local schools, including Eastvale Elementary School and Corona High School. While at Oregon State College in Corvallis, he fell in love with Lucille Van Loan, and they eloped in 1932 just before she graduated. They moved back to Eastvale, and Fred completed his undergraduate education at Pomona College. Hoping to become a journalist, Fred went to work for the *Corona Independent*, but the Great Depression soon ended his employment. He worked on the ranch with his father until 1937, when his daughter Lynne was four years old, and he was offered a position with the *Los Angeles Times*. Fred and Lucille moved to Santa Monica with their young daughter.

Fred was in the Army Reserves and was called to duty for a year in 1940. He was stationed at Fort Ord. His wife and daughter moved with him to Monterey Bay, where the fort is located. Just a year later, the bombing of Pearl Harbor thrust the United States fully into World War II. Fred was assigned to the staff of General "Vinegar Joe" Stillwell in the China-Burma-India theater, where he established the *C.B.I. Roundup* troop newspaper. He later was stationed in Paris where he worked for *Stars and Stripes*, the official newspaper of the United States Armed Forces, before returning to the States.

Fred's daughter Lynne still has a letter her grandfather wrote to her father near the end of World War II. William related news of the ranch to Fred, mentioning that he was making progress in pulling out the walnut trees. The letter said, "Things on the ranch are about as usual. Have pulled all our Payne walnuts and now have a hell of a job getting them out of the field and getting them cut up. We haul each tree to the gravel pit and dismember it there. This saves picking up and hauling the brush and stumps separately to the pit." When he was done, the only walnut trees left on the ranch were the ones around the little house where the Scamaras lived.

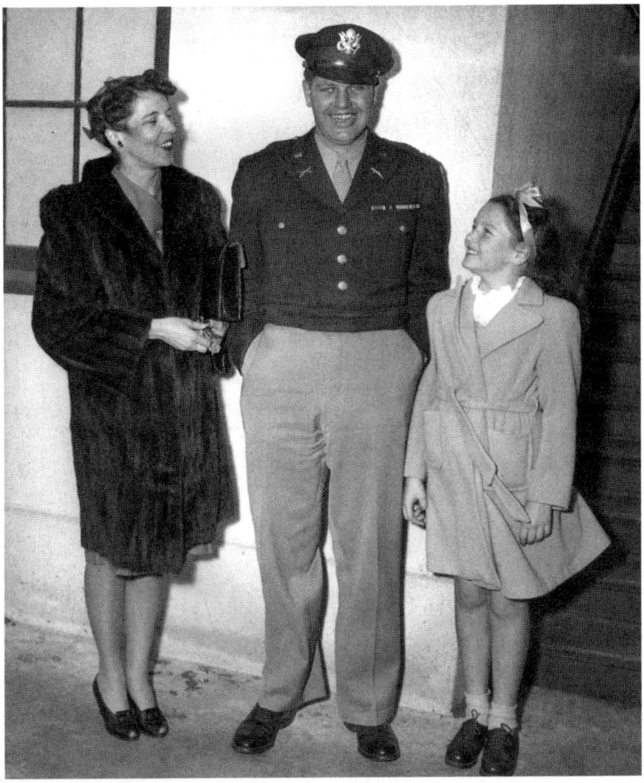

Lucille, Fred and Lynne Eldridge during World War II. *Courtesy Lynne Eldridge Richie.*

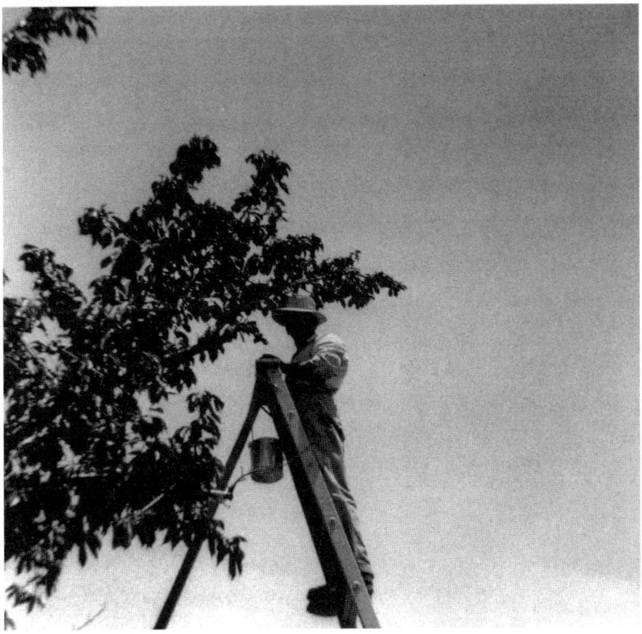

Lloyd Salgado Sr. picks walnuts from the top of a Payne walnut tree on Premier Ranch, circa 1953. *Courtesy Susan Scamara.*

Lynne relates that after Fred returned from the war, he was not interested in returning to work at a large company. He wanted to be more independent. Fred and his family moved to the nearby city of Riverside, and Fred began a career in ranch work once again at Premier Ranch.

Lynne recalls that her grandmother, Maude Eldridge, was always concerned about one particular point on the ten-mile route between Riverside and the ranch that Fred traveled every day. There was (and still is) a train crossing north of Pedley where Bellegrave Avenue crosses the Union Pacific mainline tracks at a forty-five-degree angle. The unlighted crossing, which had no warning markers or signals, was especially dangerous at night, when long freight trains were unlit except at their widely separated ends. Maude often warned Fred to be careful at the crossing, and at her insistence, the County of Riverside agreed to improve lighting there.

When William was seventy-one years old and Maude was sixty-eight, her premonitions were realized with tragic consequences. On the evening of 15

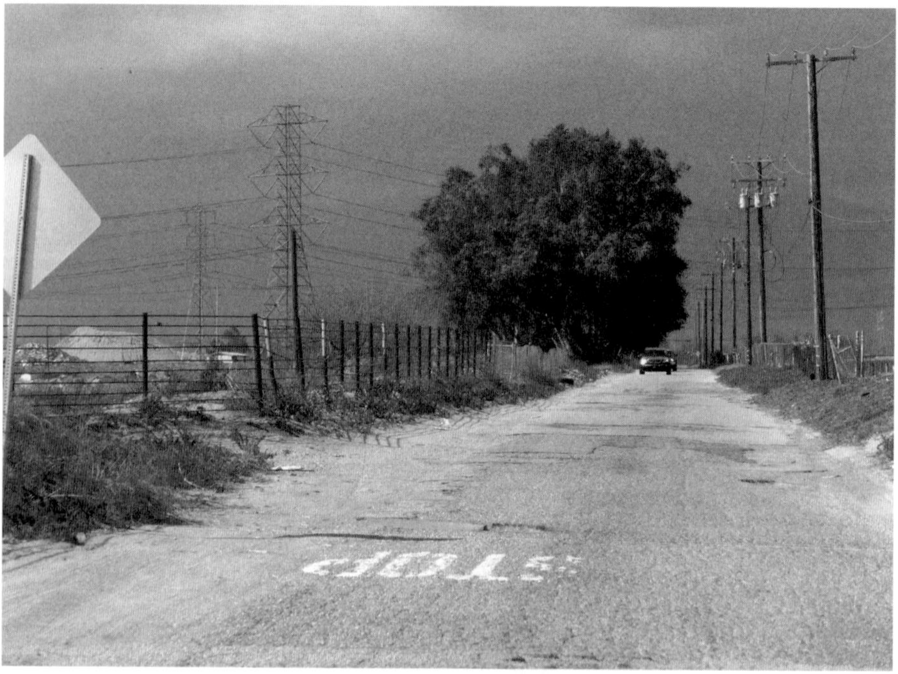

This portion of Sumner Avenue, just north of the county line in San Bernardino County, is a 2013 reminder of Eastvale road conditions from days gone by. The narrow roadway is lined by eucalyptus trees. The sign warns motorists that the roadway is subject to flooding. Kim Jarrell Johnson photo, 2013.

February 1950, William and Maude were returning home from a visit to their son and his family in Riverside. The crossing was still unlit, and they did not see the moving freight train until too late. The train dragged their car and threw it 150 feet into a field. Maude died five days later at Riverside Community Hospital. William was seriously injured, and at first, he was not expected to survive. Even after his release from the hospital several months later, he was unable to continue managing the ranch, so Fred, Lucille and their daughter Lynne moved to the ranch from Riverside so Fred could manage the ranch full time. William Eldridge died four years later.

Tom Patterson has described Fred Eldridge's 1956 venture into politics. Fred announced his candidacy in the Republican primary race for Congress

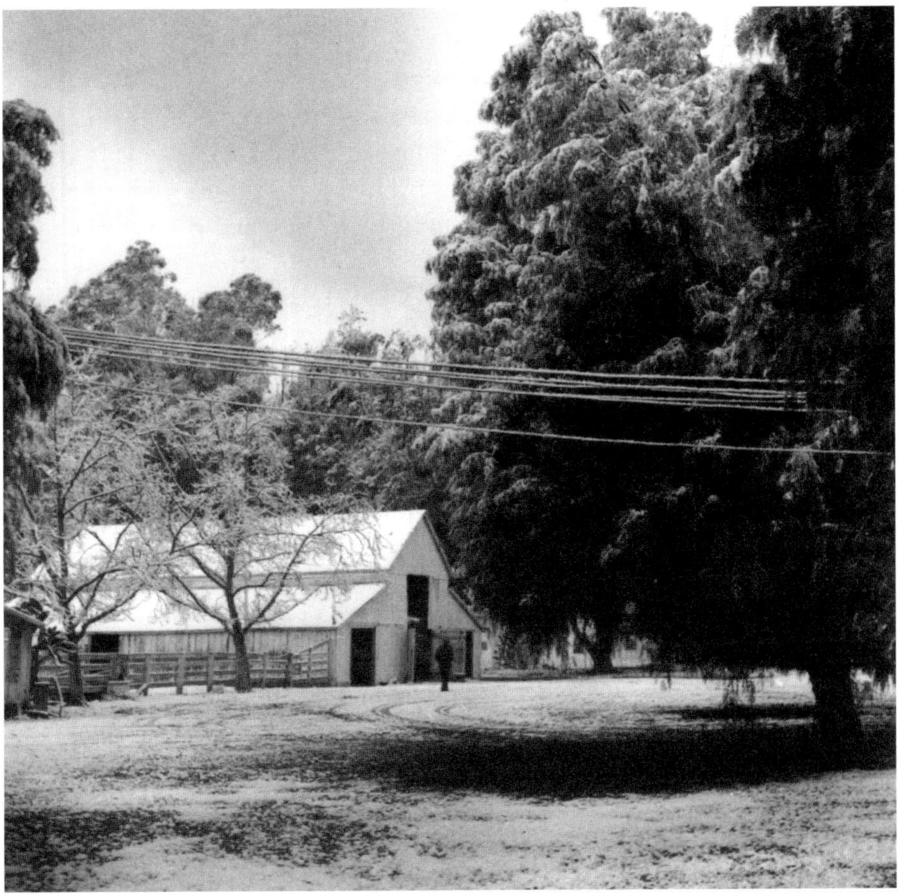

Barn on Premier Ranch on a frosty winter morning. *Courtesy Lynne Eldridge Richie.*

from California's Twenty-ninth District, which then comprised Riverside and Imperial Counties. His principal opponent in the primary was Jacqueline Cochran, who had become famous as a female aviator and was married to financier Floyd Odlum. Fred lost the primary election, but there was speculation that he remained popular enough to help split the Republican vote in the general election, which Cochran-Odlum lost to naturalized India native Dalip Singh Saund, the first Asian elected to the U.S. Congress.

In 1959, Fred Eldridge sold the ranch his father had purchased forty-eight years earlier. After a few years off for travel and relaxation, Fred purchased the *Corona Independent* in 1963. He had the best of both worlds. He was back in the newspaper business, but he was still his own boss.

The Harada Family

Fred Eldridge sold Premier Ranch in 1959 to Masaru "Speed" and Iwao "George" Harada, sons of Japanese immigrants Kiichi and Rui Harada.

Kiichi Harada was born in 1878 and came to the United States in 1904. Rui Iyemoto (sometimes spelled Kemoto) was born in 1892 and arrived from Japan in 1915. They were married in the United States and had eight children, all of whom were given Japanese names but later adopted American nicknames. Yoshio "John" was born in 1916, Masaru "Speed" in 1918, daughter Hisaye "Kita" in 1920, Iwao "George" in 1923, Takeshi "James" in 1925, Harue "Mary" in 1927, son Kenji "Ken" in 1932 and Hiroka "Peggy" in 1935. The family became vegetable farmers in Downey, about ten miles southeast of downtown Los Angeles.

In 1942, during World War II, residents of Japanese descent were involuntarily relocated, usually incurring considerable financial loss. The Harada family was sent to an assembly center at the Santa Anita racetrack where, for six months, they lived in a horse stall. The family was then sent to an internment camp in Rohwer, Arkansas. Speed, at age twenty-four, joined the U.S. Army as a member of the famed 442nd Regimental Combat Team, composed almost entirely of soldiers of Japanese descent, which came to be known as the most decorated army unit during the war. Older brother John opted to stay with the family during internment at Arkansas to act as head of the family, assisting Kiichi, who was severely afflicted with arthritis.

At the war's end, the Harada family returned to Los Angeles County, where they bought farmland in Norwalk and built a house. Later they purchased land in Cypress and moved the house they had built from

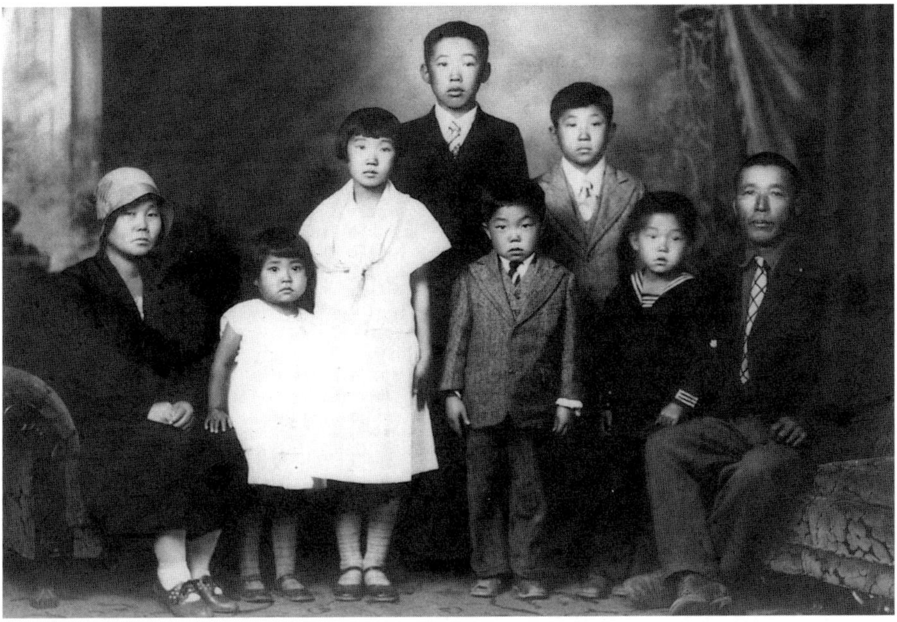

The Harada family, about 1932. *From left*: mother Rui, Harue (Mary), Hisaye (Kita), Yoshio (John), Iwao (George), Masaru (Speed), Tadashi (James) and father Kiichi. The two youngest children were not yet born when this photo was taken. *Courtesy Harada Family.*

Norwalk to Cypress. As the Cypress area developed and farmland converted to postwar housing tracts, Speed and George went looking for a place to relocate their farm.

They found property they wanted to buy in rural Eastvale. They bought Premier Ranch in late 1959 and moved there in January 1960. Speed's daughter JoAnn, who was twelve when they came to Eastvale, recalls that she thought her new home was "out in the middle of nowhere." There were no signals at any of the street intersections. She had never before experienced strong Santa Ana winds, which blew in full force across the open agricultural lands of Eastvale. The main landmark on Hamner Avenue was the Huddle (later Al's Corner), a bar located at Schleisman Road that was useful as a point of reference for visitors from outside the area.

Speed, his wife, Hisako "Mary," and their six children, along with mother Rui, moved into the adobe house. (Kiichi had died in 1957.) Daughter JoAnn remembers being impressed by the size and style of their new home.

The house that had been moved from Cypress to Norwalk was moved again to the farm in Eastvale. John, the eldest Harada son, had died in a car

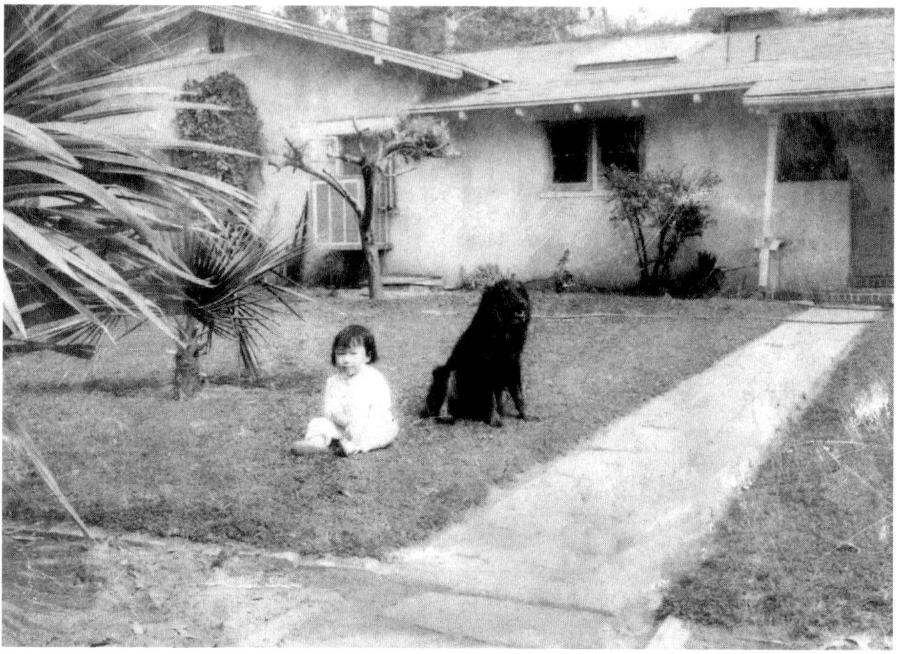

Little Gloria Harada, daughter of Speed, sits in front of the adobe house with the family dog, circa 1965. *Courtesy Harada Family.*

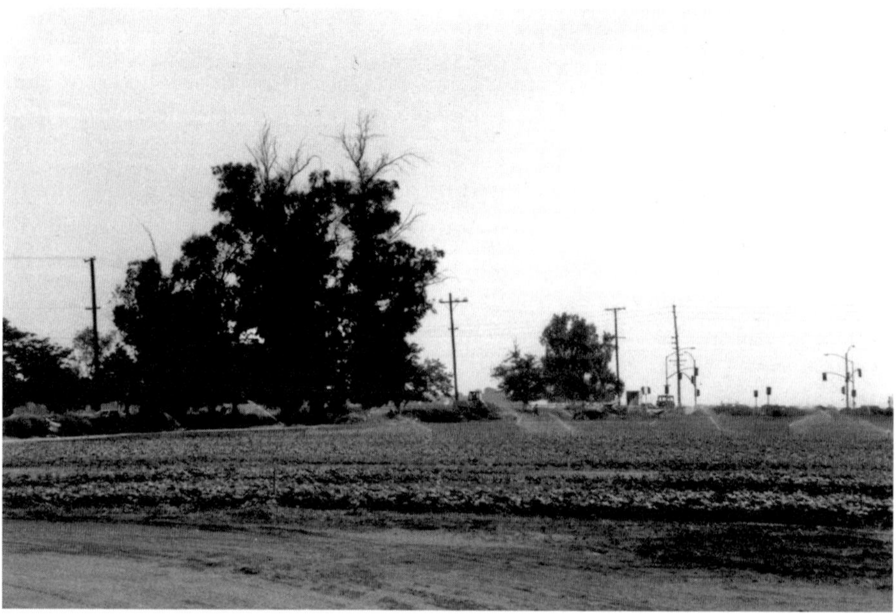

The intersection of Limonite Avenue (formerly Cloverdale Road) and Hamner Avenue can be seen across Harada farm fields in the 1970s. *Courtesy Harada Family.*

accident in 1956, and in 1960, his widow, Yoshiko "Yo," married George. George moved with his new wife and her four young children to the house that was moved onto the property. George and Yo later added a child of their own to the family.

The Harada family raised vegetables on their new property. In summer they grew corn, cabbage and onions, and in winter they raised cauliflower and broccoli. They sold the vegetables primarily at the wholesale market in Los Angeles. The Haradas devoted part of the property to a feedlot where they raised beef cattle. They also raised alfalfa on the ranch.

Everyone in the family pitched in to get work done on the ranch. George ran the farm as the overall manager. Speed was in charge of spraying the fields, and he did the cultivating, ground preparation and harvesting. He also did mechanical work on the ranch. The older Harada boys drove the trucks full of vegetables into the Los Angeles market. JoAnn Gunter remembered that everyone did whatever needed to be done. Additional workers, usually Hispanic, were hired to assist with farm work as well.

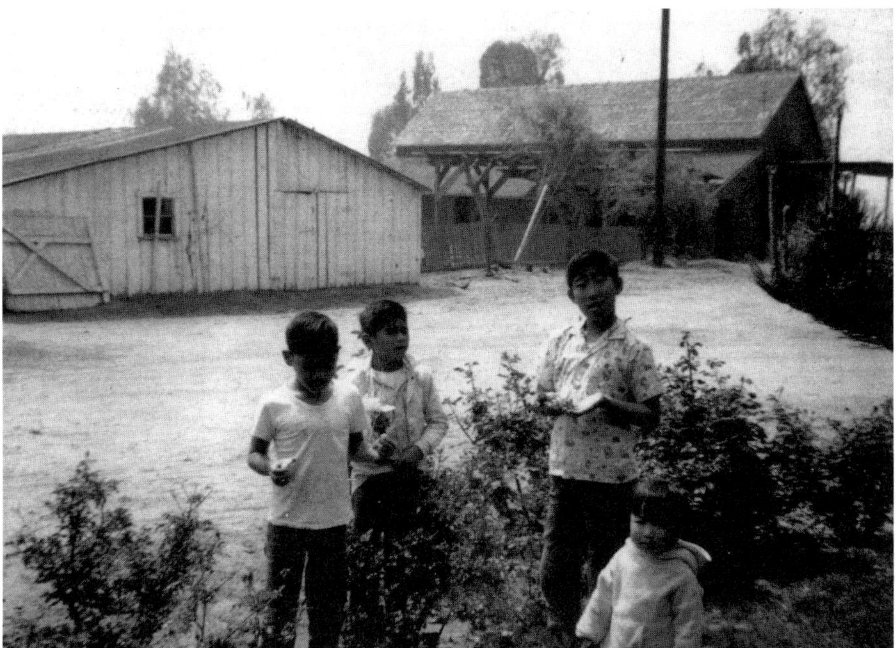

From left to right: Leonard Harada, Albino (son of a ranch worker), Gordon Harada and Gloria Harada on the ranch, circa 1965. The barn at the right in the background had stood on the property since it was owned by the Eldridge family. *Courtesy Harada Family.*

George and Speed's brother James, his wife, Violet, and their family also lived on the ranch and ran an egg operation known as Jim's Poultry Ranch. During the ten years from 1960 to 1970, the egg ranch grew to include one hundred thousand chickens. Violet was usually the candler, worked as the poultry ranch's bookkeeper and did anything else that needed to be done. Later James moved the egg ranch to property he purchased in Chino, where the operation grew to include one million birds.

JoAnn remembers, "It was amazing as I look back on how my mom and my aunts worked, they worked so hard and still kept up the household duties of washing, cleaning and cooking. I always said that my mom worked circles around me."

Many people worked with or for the Harada family over the years and came to respect and appreciate them. One such story comes from Loren's wife, Peggy Meissner. Mary Kennedy lived at Riverdale Acres and was a close friend of Loren's mother-in-law, Dessie Pritchard. When the Harada family purchased Premier Ranch, Mary was hired as a permanent housekeeper for Yo. Mary didn't drive a car, but she liked to walk, and Yo's house was about a mile and a half from where Mary lived, so Mary walked across on Limonite sometimes, but at other times, Yo came and got her or Dessie took her to the Harada farm. After a few years, Dessie had become well acquainted with Yo Harada. Dessie found that the Harada family, and especially Yo, were very generous. They treated Mary well, and they usually took her along when they went on vacations, as a paid helper but also to let her enjoy the outings. The Harada family had a reputation for being community oriented and cooperative.

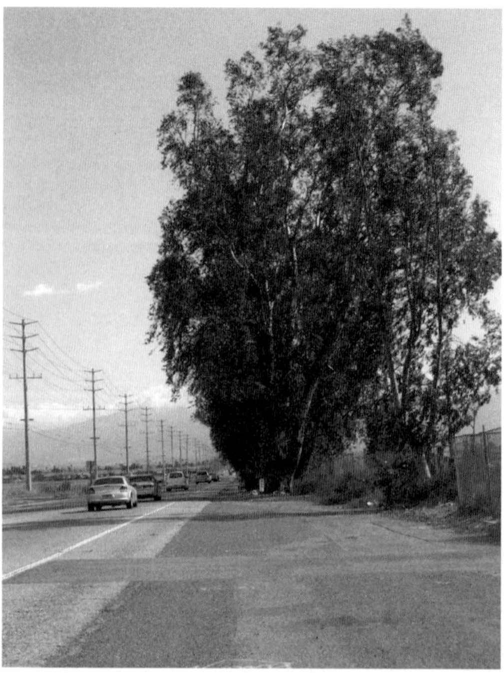

Part of Hamner Avenue is still lined with tall eucalyptus trees, as it has been for more than fifty years. Kim Jarrell Johnson photo, 2013.

When Dessie died in 1997, Mary Kennedy wanted to attend her funeral, and Yo

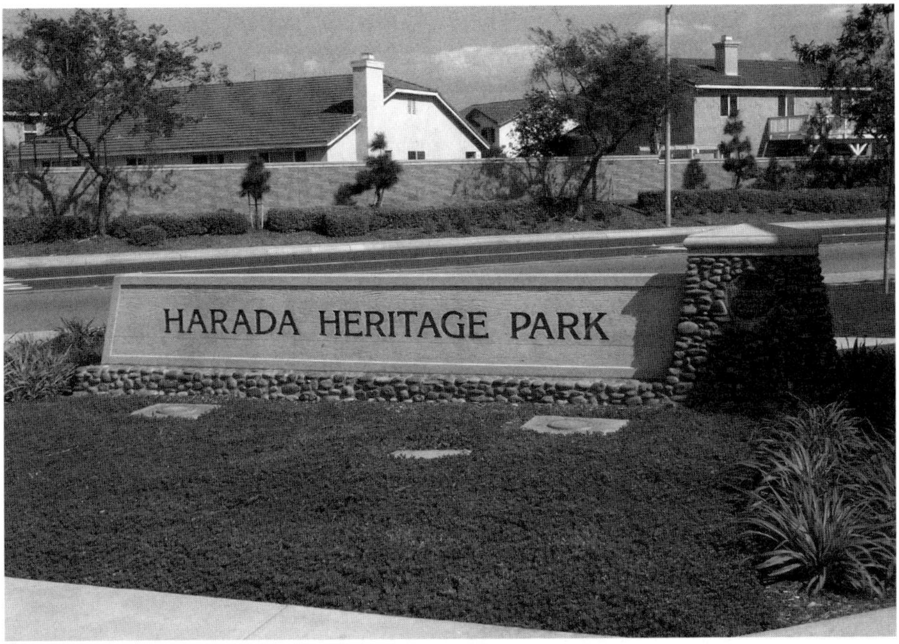

Harada Heritage Park commemorates the Harada family's long association with Eastvale. Kim Jarrell Johnson photo, 2013.

brought her, because of Yo's respect for Dessie, with whom she had become acquainted, and to provide transportation to the funeral for Mary.

Speed and his wife, Mary, retired from the farm about 1985 and moved near their daughter JoAnn Gunter at Riverdale Acres in Mira Loma. George continued to live at the farm while members of the younger generation took over the farming operation. The family began selling land to residential developers in about 1990. Harada Heritage Park in Eastvale, named for the Harada family, was dedicated at the corner of Sixty-fifth Street and Scholar Way. The Harada family retained ownership in a piece of property that is still occupied (as of 2013) by one of George's children. Speed died in 1995, and George followed in 2009.

5.5 A LATER VIEW

Loren remembers that his first real job, during the summer of 1944 following his junior year of high school, was on a farm. It was located on Merrill Avenue west of Archibald and just north of the Eastvale boundary. Alfalfa

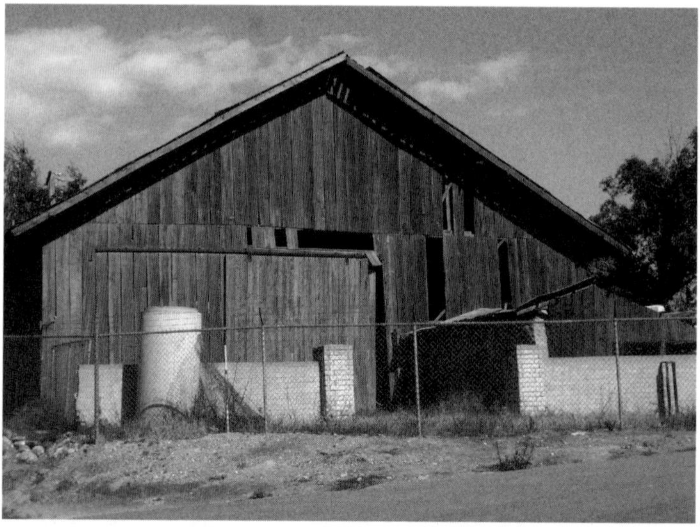

This old barn is a reminder of bygone days. It could still be seen on Fifty-eighth Street in April 2013. Kim Jarrell Johnson photo, 2013.

was one of the main crops. At harvest time, mowed alfalfa was raked into long rows that had to be baled early the following day to retain moisture, essential to the curing process. On days when baling was scheduled, he mounted his bike at dawn and rode three miles from home to the field. The gasoline-powered baler was pulled by a mule. More experienced farm workers pitched alfalfa in to be pressed into bales while Loren tied the baling wire and guided the mule. By 9:00 or 10:00 a.m., the day's baling quota was finished, and the mule was hitched to a wagon that hauled the baled hay into the barn.

Besides alfalfa, the farm where Loren worked grew vegetables, including black-eyed peas, potatoes and sweet corn. A problem with potatoes is the large amount of labor required for digging them. The owner of the farm was testing a digging machine somebody had invented, but he found it unsuited to the soil texture of his farm because it produced clods about the same size as potatoes, making mechanical separation difficult.

Loren and the other farm workers harvested ears of sweet corn from the stalks. A mule pulled a sled that hauled the ears to a packing table, where other workers packed them into crates. A truck picked up the crates of corn each afternoon during the season and took them to Los Angeles. At a produce auction there, the next morning before daybreak, the corn and other farm produce would be sold to retail markets.

Chapter 6

EASTVALE'S DAIRY YEARS

Dairies were a part of the Eastvale ranching landscape from very early times. Dairy cows figured prominently in the history of the Fuller Ranch (Chapter 4) and in the Premier Ranch story (Chapter 5), and other dairies were scattered across Eastvale prior to World War II. However, since most milking was done by hand at that time, dairies were limited in size, and they were often secondary to the multiple agricultural enterprises in which the large ranches were engaged.

That all changed after World War II. The postwar baby boom and subsequent building boom in Los Angeles County caused many dairy

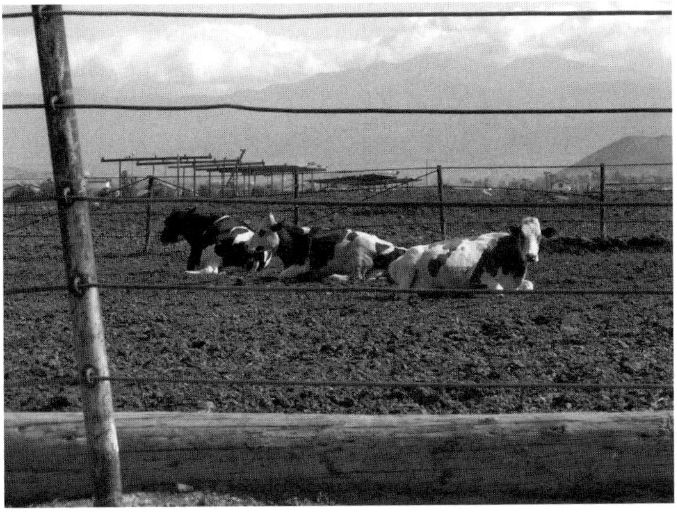

Cows relax at a dairy on Fifty-eighth Street. Only a few dairies remain in Eastvale. Kim Jarrell Johnson photo, 2013.

farmers to sell their land and move away. Many dairies located in Cerritos, Artesia and Paramount that had been started in the 1920s began to look east for land, moving first to Chino and Ontario and then to Eastvale. By the 1950s, those areas had become the center of the Southern California dairy industry.

6.1 BOOTSMA CALF RANCH

Ike Bootsma, a city council member in Eastvale, was raised on a dairy ranch in Chino. His father immigrated to America in the early 1930s from the Netherlands and worked at dairy farms in the Artesia area before buying twenty acres in Chino in 1938. There he established a dairy that, at its peak, had 250 cows. Ike was the seventh of nine children in the Bootsma family. He graduated from high school in 1964, served two years in Vietnam and then earned a degree in animal science at California State Polytechnic University–Pomona. Ike and his brother John purchased twenty acres east of Archibald and south of Schleisman in what they thought of as the far edge of Chino Valley, or maybe Corona, but not Eastvale. Eastvale was a school, not a place, as far as they knew.

The Bootsma brothers went into the calf-raising business. They planned to raise calves that they would sell to the area dairies. The calf-raising business would be their steppingstone to owning their own dairy one day. Fate and science intervened. Only six months or so after starting their business, Ike was approached by an area dairyman. He, like many dairy farmers at that time, was beginning to use genetics and investing time and energy in breeding his dairy cows to get a superior milk producer. The dairyman didn't want to sell his calves to Ike and then turn around and have to buy inferior calves later. But, at the same time, raising calves is very time and labor intensive. The dairyman proposed that the Bootsma Calf Ranch raise his calves for him.

According to Ike Bootsma, the first four months of a dairy calf's life are very labor intensive for the farmer, as well as the riskiest time of the calf's

Opposite, bottom: This aerial photo of the Bootsma Calf Ranch was taken in the early 2000s. At the bottom left of the photo is the Bootsma home. Behind the home are holding ponds for water runoff from the calf pens. Behind the ponds are corrals where the older calves were kept. At the top of the photo are calf boxes, where baby calves were kept for their first ten weeks on the ranch. *Courtesy Ike Bootsma.*

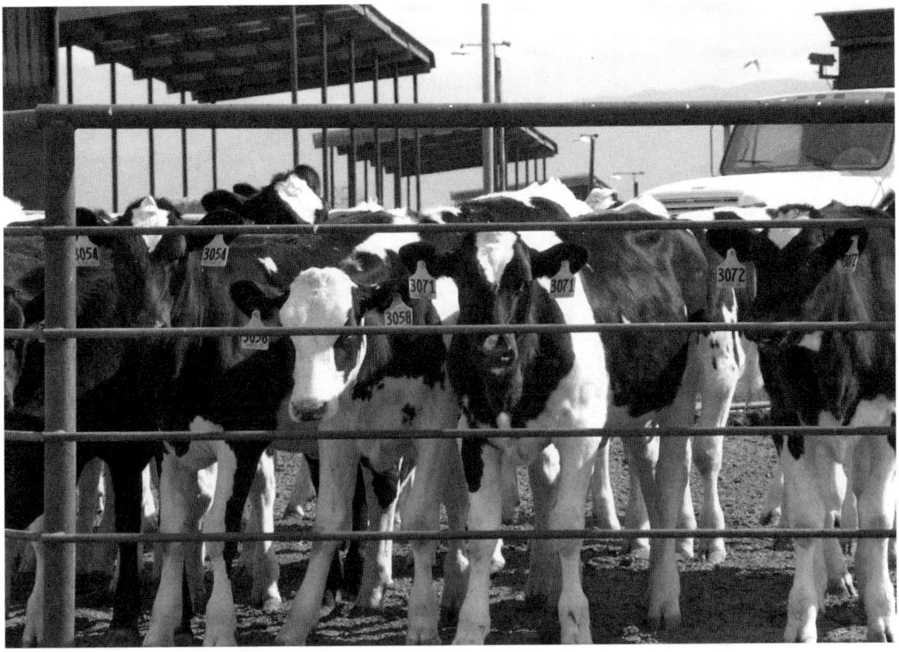

Curious calves on Eucalyptus Avenue crowd around the fence to see a car go by in April 2013. Kim Jarrell Johnson photo, 2013.

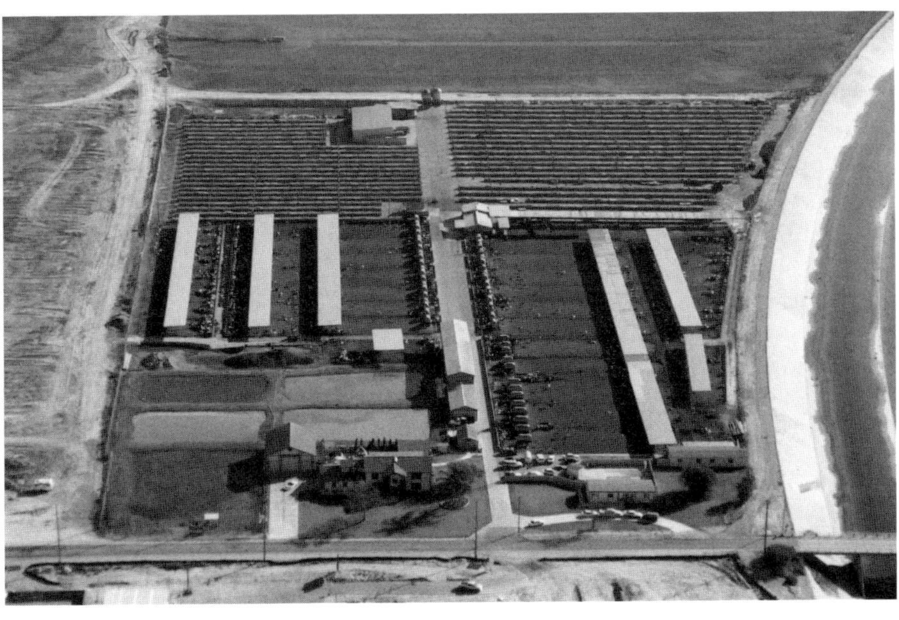

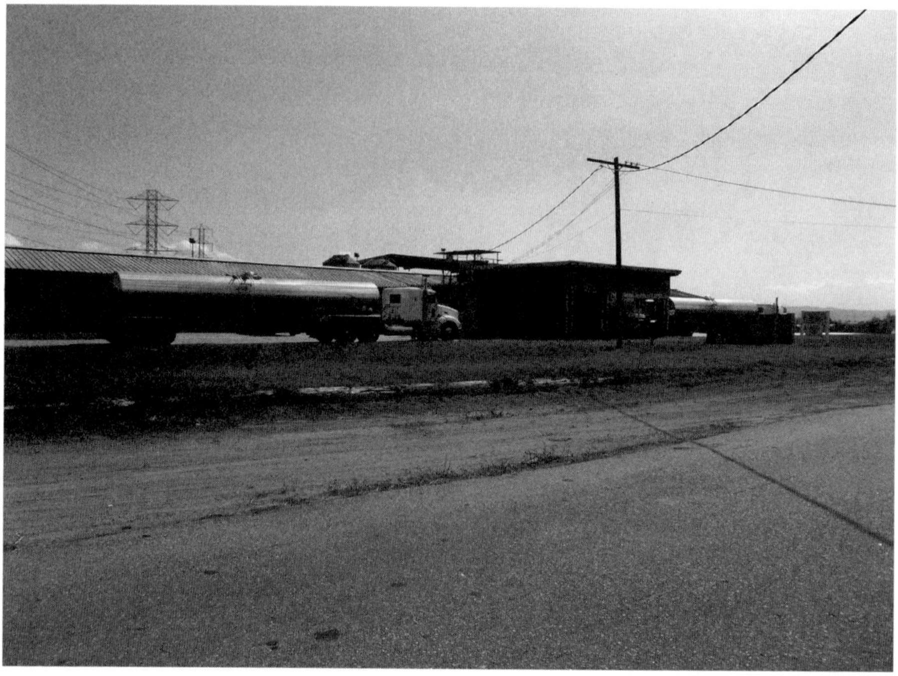

A tank truck loads milk at one of Eastvale's last dairies in April 2013. Kim Jarrell Johnson photo, 2013.

life. The calves have to be bottle-fed three times a day for the first ten weeks of their lives. The Bootsma Calf Ranch would collect calves every day from area ranches. They would raise them for four months and then return them to the ranches where they came from. At its peak, the ranch had 8,500 calves at any one time and employed thirty-two people.

According to Ike, most of the dairies in the Eastvale area were owned by Dutch immigrants, with a few owned by Portuguese immigrants. The milkers were all either Portuguese or Basque immigrants who had a background in milking. The laborers on the dairy ranches who fixed fences and took care of the corrals were usually Mexican immigrants.

Eastvale was really a small community where everyone knew everyone, according to Ike and his wife, Squeaker. Squeaker said there wasn't much traffic back in the 1970s and '80s, but what traffic there was usually consisted of big trucks. Trucks were always hauling in hay and grain and hauling out milk. Cows were also often transported in and out of Eastvale in large trucks.

6.2 THE VAN LEEUWENS

A 2006 article in the *Los Angeles Times* highlighted another Eastvale family, the Van Leeuwens. Eastvale dairy farmer Bill Van Leeuwen's grandfather moved to Paramount in Los Angeles County from the Netherlands in the late 1920s. He opened a small dairy, where he milked sixty cows each day by hand.

In 1945, Van Leeuwen's father purchased seventeen acres in Norwalk, where he had a herd of 180 cows. The new dairy used mechanical milking machines. But the post–World War II building boom made Van Leeuwen's father feel fenced in, and he sold the Norwalk dairy land for $17,000 and moved to Chino in 1957.

Twenty years later, Bill Van Leeuwen went out on his own and purchased 131 acres in the Eastvale area, where he milked 1,600 cows. As land values rose, the family saw yet another opportunity to sell and expand. Van Leeuwen sold 40 acres to a developer in 2004 for more than $10 million. According to Van Leeuwen, dairy farmers "will say they were forced out by urbanization, but really we were enticed to leave." Van Leeuwen also said something that residents of Eastvale's first subdivisions might agree with: "People and cows don't mix."

6.3 PEOPLE FROM ALL OVER THE WORLD

People from all over the world were attracted to the dairy industry in the Chino Valley, and many came to Eastvale. The resulting multicultural population created a unique situation at Eastvale Elementary School. Dutch, Basque, Mexican and Portuguese children, many who had parents who did not speak English, all attended the school. The school honored these cultures by celebrating holidays and customs from their students' native lands. The Mexican custom of Las Posadas was celebrated in December. Three Kings Day in January was celebrated as it would be in Portugal and elsewhere in Europe. Every May, the school had International Day when students would come dressed in the native costumes of their Mexican, Basque, Dutch or Portuguese homelands.

Due to its proximity to so many dairies, the school had to include information in the teachers' manual that other schools did not require. One part of the manual addressed "cow alerts." This provided a procedure that teachers were required to follow if the cows stampeded and broke through the fence surrounding the school.

Portuguese immigrant dairy workers had a particularly large presence in Eastvale during the dairy years. An area basically north of Chandler Street, between Archibald and Hellman Avenues, had been subdivided before 1915 by the Persimmon Acres Tract. Over time, people built houses on those lots, and a number of the houses were occupied by the Portuguese dairy workers. So many of them lived there that it became known as "Portugee Village."

Squeaker Bootsma remembers parades and festivals going on in Portugee Village, with traditional foods such as roast goat being prepared. She even remembers Portugee Village having its own small version of the running of the bulls. At the end of a short dirt road off Walters Street, someone built a large shrine out of smooth river rock, which included a four- or five-foot statue of the Virgin Mary. The parades commemorating religious events would often stop at the shrine. According to one of Portugee Village's residents, the shrine was removed several years ago to accommodate a wall that went up around an adjacent housing development.

6.4 Swan Lake

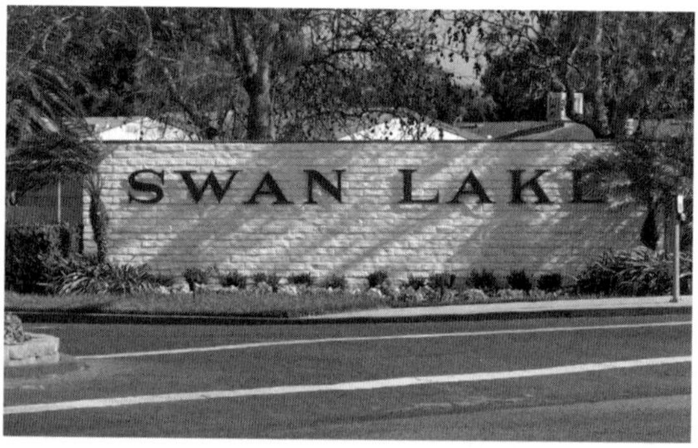

Entrance to Swan Lake Mobile Home Park on Hamner Avenue. Kim Jarrell Johnson photo, 2013.

During the 1960s at the beginning of the true "dairy era" in Eastvale, a somewhat surprising land development was proposed by private developers and was approved by the County of Riverside. Swan Lake, a 126-acre mobile home community just east of Hamner Avenue and north of Limonite Avenue, was founded for senior-only housing. It existed for almost three decades as an enclave of fairly dense development in the midst of the dairies. Many years later, the age restriction was terminated, and Swan Lake became relatively low-cost housing for hundreds of families.

Chapter 7

EASTVALE ENTERS THE TWENTY-FIRST CENTURY

7.1 The Influence of Interstate 15

As early as the late 1940s, it became clear that a freeway route was needed that would run north and south though inland Southern California, connecting Cajon Pass with Temecula and thence with San Diego. Meanwhile, the freeway would cross several heavily traveled east–west roads between Corona and Cucamonga that provided commuter routes between inland "bedroom communities" and coastal work sites.

Serious study produced a proposal for the Interstate 15 connection that would involve Temescal Canyon south and east of Corona. From Corona, the obvious connection to Cajon Pass would bypass the La Sierra hills through Norco and cross the Santa Ana River near Eastvale. As plans for the new freeway became more firm during the 1950s, it soon became obvious that there was no route through Norco that was without controversy. Due to the topography, a route west of Hamner would be prohibitively expensive, but many local residents felt that a route east of Hamner would split the Norco community and disrupt its rural lifestyle. Debate on the issue was quite heated and delayed construction of that portion of I-15 for at least a decade.

While folks in Eastvale may have been involved in those debates, it was a Norco issue for the most part. Eastvale was affected, of course, but there were few barriers to construction north of the river. The alignment of what came to be named Interstate 15 through Eastvale was decided by the debate in Norco. The eastern route was the winner, and the route through Eastvale was set.

7.2 Growing Pains

Eastvale was very rural and sparsely populated in 1955 at the start of the Norco debates and was still primarily agricultural land even after 1976, when demolition for I-15 construction began. However, Riverside County planners could see that the freeway would likely induce relocation of the many dairies in Eastvale and the development of that land with houses and shopping centers. The Riverside County Planning Department included the Eastvale Community Plan in its comprehensive General Plan, in anticipation of the expected growth. Remember that, until incorporation of Eastvale as a city in October 2010, planning was deferred to agencies no closer to the community than at the Riverside County level.

Meanwhile, construction on the freeway continued, and the portion of I-15 through Eastvale and Norco, between the U.S. 60 and U.S. 91 freeways, was completed and opened for use in June 1989. Alert residents were beginning to realize that the future was almost at hand.

A small portion of Eastvale fell within the Jurupa Area Recreation and Parks District, but no existing park district was in place to take ownership of and maintain the parks in the majority of Eastvale that would be constructed in conjunction with the anticipated future housing developments. In 1996, the Jurupa Community Services District, the water and sewer provider for the Eastvale area (as well as most of the Pedley, Mira Loma and Glen Avon areas of the city of Jurupa Valley), agreed to take on the park management task for Eastvale. The district developed and approved a park plan for the community.

7.3 Forming a Community

The first subdivision to be built was the Cloverdale Farms development, later known as Cloverdale Farms I, by Lewis Homes. It was located at the southwest corner of Hamner Avenue and Cloverdale Road (as that section of Limonite Avenue was then called), behind the shopping center

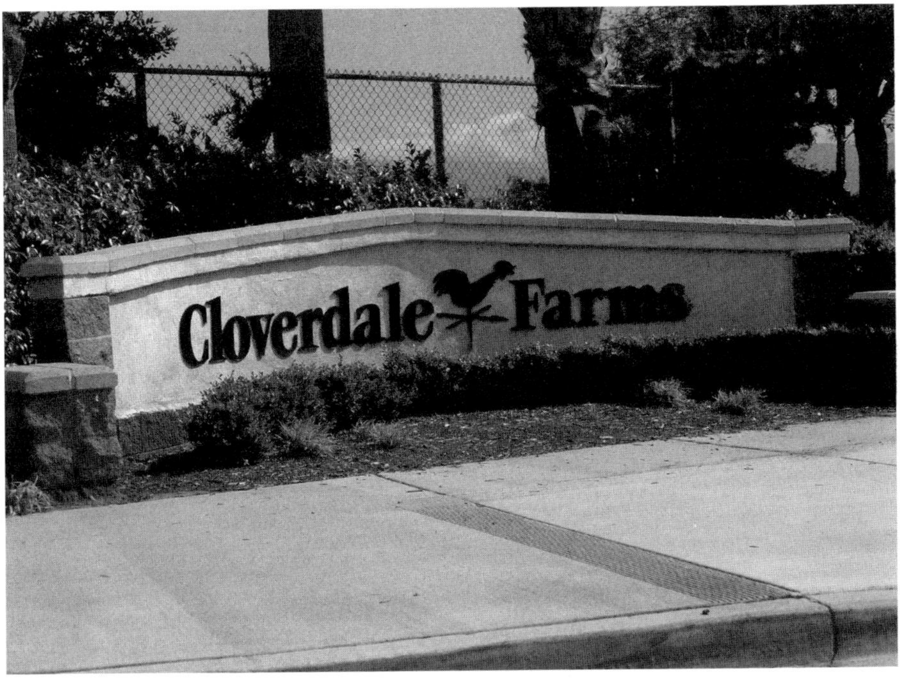

This monument marks the entrance to Cloverdale Farms residential tract, opened in 1999. Kim Jarrell Johnson photo, 2013.

that is located on that corner today, on the former site of Premier Ranch. Residents began moving into the tract in 1999. Jane Anderson, one of the first residents to buy a home and move into that tract, recalls that traffic control at the corner of Hamner and Limonite consisted of three stop signs. The only retail establishment close to the new development was Al's Corner at Schleisman Road, a bar that had formerly been known as the Huddle.

In 2001, a group of Eastvale residents formed the Eastvale Community Committee (ECC) to address issues in their area. They contacted Supervisor John Tavaglione's office and then held their first meeting in the driveway of Mike and Jane Anderson's home. Seventy-five people from a total of 209 homes attended that first meeting. Later, in fall 2003, the ECC started a community newsletter called the *Eastvale Edition*, which published a summary of information from the community meetings as well as other information for Eastvale residents.

Residents of Eastvale looked forward to shopping in their own community. The Eastvale Gateway retail center was constructed north of Limonite Avenue, between Hamner Avenue and Interstate 15, where Home Depot was the first store to open in late 2003.

7.4 Onward to Cityhood

In October 2006, the residents of the Jurupa Valley area began exploring the idea of incorporation. Some residents of Eastvale realized that those cityhood plans included at least a portion of the Eastvale area. This spurred them to action. In spring 2007, a group of Eastvale residents formed the Eastvale Incorporation Committee and started the arduous three-year process that culminated on 21 January 2010, when the Riverside County Local Agency Formation Commission (LAFCO) approved the application for incorporation to go forward to a vote of Eastvale residents.

The incorporation vote was held on 8 June 2010. Of those who voted in the election, 68.5 percent voted in favor of cityhood. In that same election, voters selected Eastvale's first city council: Ike Bootsma, Jeff DeGrandpre, Kelly Howell, Adam Rush and Ric Welsh.

The new city council–elect had just four months to create the structure for the new city, whose official incorporation date was 1 October 2010. The council-elect selected Adam Rush as Eastvale's first mayor and Jeff DeGrandpre as mayor pro tem.

On 1 October 2010 a celebration of Eastvale's incorporation as the twenty-seventh city in California was held in the stadium at Eleanor Roosevelt High School. It included a parade, presentations and fireworks. The new residents of Eastvale could now take charge of their own destiny.

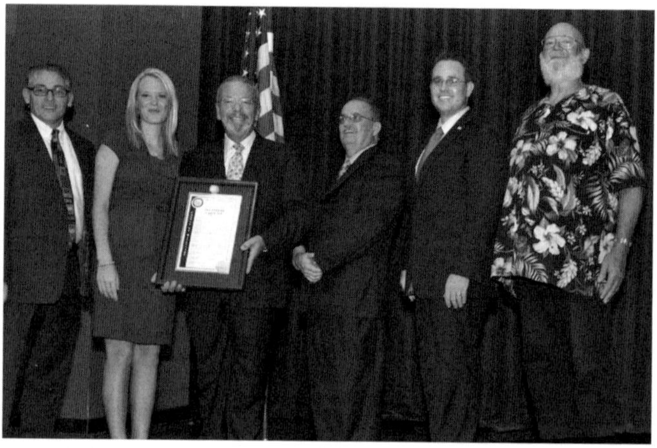

County Supervisor John Tavaglione presented a plaque to the first Eastvale city council at the Inaugural Celebration on 1 October 2010. *From left:* Rick Welch, Kelly Howell, John Tavaglione, Jeff DeGrandpre, Adam Rush and Ike Bootsma. *Courtesy City of Eastvale.*

Appendix A

EXCERPTS FROM "ARCADIA AND THE FORGOTTEN GUAPA,"

BY WALTER T. GARNER

This appendix is excerpted from a document written about 1940 by Walter Taylor Garner (1877–1949) that was transcribed in 1967 and reprinted in 1981. Bound copies of the transcription are available from Jurupa Mountains Cultural Center in Jurupa Valley, north of Mission Boulevard between Glen Avon and Sunnyslope.

An introduction, bound with the transcription, tells how the center acquired Garner's document. Louis Thomas, a local Riverside and Jurupa historian, met Cecil Galloway at the center. Galloway "provided the Center Museum with considerable information about the area. Among the thoughtful gifts to the Center Museum was an original document written by Walter T. Garner about 1930." It must have been written somewhat later, however, since it mentions the 1938 flood that washed away the Hamner Avenue bridge at Norco.

ARCADIA AND THE FORGOTTEN GUAPA

In my childhood I heard strange tales of the Guapa, also called the Guapia or Juapa, a district located in the river valley of the Santa Ana River. It extended from the point where the bridge now crosses the stream on the road to Arlington *[Pedley Road bridge near De Anza Narrows, replaced after 1938 by Van Buren Boulevard bridge]*, in a southwesterly direction to a point some distance below the Auburndale bridge on the road between Chino and Corona.

In the year 1838, Juan Bandini made claim to Jurupa Grant, which included the Guapa or Juapa.

Juan Bandini had a daughter, the fair, the beautiful, the kind and thoughtful Arcadia. *[See Chapter 1.]* She was "the apple of his eye." He built her a house on the bluff, a splendid house for that time. This was the first house on the Guapa and was Bandini's headquarters on Jurupa, the official name of the grant. In after years as you stood on the river flats, where the squatters had once had their homes, and looked up at the bluffs, you could see the broken walls of the old Bandini adobe where Arcadia had lived as a girl.

A.1 Guapa Rancho and Guapa Springs

Jane Davies Gunther in Riverside County Place Names *(1984) begins, as does Garner, with a broader description of Guapa as a San Gabriel Mission ranch district, during the Mission era prior to Mexican independence in 1822 and probably even earlier as an Indian settlement. But the name came to be best known as applied to the springs, a popular rest stop on the Old Spanish Trail.*

According to Garner, the springs of Guapa were located where Cucamonga Creek "comes through the bluff." This is consistent with other documents, especially the 1888 irrigation map that shows "ciénegas" flowing into a dam and gristmill (also mentioned elsewhere) on Cucamonga Creek near its junction with the Santa Ana River.

The Guapa as a Mission Rancho

By 1822, the Guapa had become a Mission Rancho. The first mention of the place, which was to become one of the wealthier ranchos of the Mission San Gabriel, was made in the diary of Father José Sanchez. As he was exploring the interior of Southern California in 1821, he and his party, as they were riding from San Bernardino Asistencia to San Gabriel, stopped and rested at a place called Guapa.

The second mention of the name is in 1822 when Father Payeros referred to Guapa as being six leagues from the station of San Bernardino.

The center of the rancho was near two large springs which made a fine stream at that time, but are very weak now. The springs are located where the storm drain of the Cucamonga wash comes through the bluff.

These are the springs of Guapa.

The first road or trail came into the valley near what is now Pomona and skirted the foot of the Chino Hills to the point where the end of Euclid is now. It then turned more to the east and followed the valley of the Santa Ana River to the Asistencia *[at present-day Redlands]*. In following the road, the early travelers were always near wood, grass, and water.

The Old Spanish Road

The first road or trail that came into the valley was a very roundabout road, but, after the Asistencia was built *[1819]*, the Spanish army made a more direct road across the Cucamonga Desert by way of what is now the northern part of Pomona. This road crossed Euclid Avenue in Ontario near where Chaffey College is now located *[approximating present-day I-10]*. The main road went on in a southeasterly direction to the northern slope of the Jurupa Hills *[south of Fontana]*, where the Declez quarry is now located. It was then called "Point of the Hill," and any person on the hill could view the road for a great distance in either direction. There were springs in the hills which furnished some water for those traveling, but they were not very large. The road passed along the northern slope of the hills to the valley of the Santa Ana River *[at Colton]*. There it joined the first, or river, road. It then followed the river valley to the Asistencia of San Bernardino.

A.2 Old Bandini House Site at Present-Day Eastvale

Bandini's first house at present-day Eastvale is mentioned in the record of the December 1838 Jurupa land grant survey. Some recent descriptions confuse this house with the Bandini-Cota Adobe a few miles farther west on El Rincón grant or even with the Robidoux house constructed much later and much farther east on Rancho Jurupa.

Garner's description of the location of the Old Bandini House, and the relics he observed at the site, is fairly consistent with George William Beattie's October 1931 letter to Corona historian Janet Williams Gould, located at the Corona Library's Heritage Room. The house was at the edge of the bluff north of the river, west of present-day Eastvale Fire Station, but documents vary with regard to the distance from Hamner Avenue.

Garner describes the site as five hundred feet west of Hamner and close enough to be totally obliterated during reconstruction of the road after the 1938 flood. In contrast, the inscription on Gould's 1933 memorial marker located the site three thousand feet west.

This number was based on Beattie's statement, in his October 1931 letter to Gould, that he found the ruins about one thousand yards southwest of Hamner. Beattie's letter, in turn, might have referred to a prior conversation with Garner: "I can tell you where traces of what were pointed out to me as the Bandini house and its belongings were found."

Garner's 500-feet figure seems consistent with the "House" marked on Hancock's 1856 survey map, which appears very close to the Hamner alignment. Tom Patterson (1964) compromises by saying, "Historians have recently pinpointed the site as approximately 1,000 feet west of Hamner."

Bandini's First House on Rancho Jurupa

In order to receive a grant there were certain rules to be complied with. The land must be measured, a house built, the place stocked with cattle and horses; care must be given to the Indians who lived on the land, and someone must live on the place.

Juan Bandini was a very energetic man. While running the lines of his rancho, he was at the same time building his house and stocking his rancho with horses and cattle. He built his first house on the north bluff of the Santa Ana River, north of what is now Norco. The house stood about five hundred feet west of Adams Avenue *[now Hamner]* where it comes over the river bluff. It was called the Old Bandini House or the First House of Bandini.

All the water for the household needs had to be carried up the bluff. All the work that could be done was done at the lagoon at the foot of the bluff.

[Parts of the description in the two following paragraphs may reflect confusion with the Bandini-Cota Adobe on El Rincón grant, constructed within the following two years. Logs were hauled for this second Bandini house from a later grant of land in the mountains.]

The house was of adobe made on the place and of timber brought from the San Bernardino Mountains. It was about fifty feet long and twenty-five feet wide, extending north and south. It had a flat roof made of dry grass and willow branches, covered with brea (tar) from the natural tar pits.

In my youth *[about 1890]*, I knew an old Indian called Duarte, who in his boyhood days helped build the house of Bandini. He told me many things about early days; for instance, that when Bandini came from Mission San Gabriel, he brought with him many horses, cattle, and oxen, also wooden wagons on which he hauled logs from the mountains to build his house. Duarte also said there were a large number of small children in the family and that Arcadia, the eldest at about thirteen years of age, was a very intelligent young woman whom Don Juan and La Señora consulted on many things. The family were all wonderfully dressed and had many strange things, at least strange to him.

Living for some time in his first house, Bandini later built the Cota house. The old house, taken over by Bandini's servants, was kept in good repair for a number of years and people lived in it until about 1880. When the roof was later taken off to be used in building another house, the adobe soon melted down. There is nothing now to show where the house on the Guapa, the headquarters of Juan Bandini on Jurupa, once stood. And thereby hangs a tale:

According to the old stories, Juan Murietta was a nephew of the wife of José Maria Valdez, superintendent on the Cucamonga Rancho. *[Juan Murietta (1844–1936) was a peaceful shepherd whose older brother Esequial (Ezekiel) founded the town of Murietta in southwest Riverside County. They were unrelated to the semi-fictional Gold Rush–era bandit Joaquin Murietta.]* Murietta made many of his holdups on the old Spanish Road near what is now the Declez quarry. Here he could watch from the hill and see the road for some miles in both directions. He is supposed to have buried some of his stolen gold near the Old Bandini House. I myself have seen holes dug around the house by people who were seeking the buried treasure. At that time the walls were all but gone, but there was a great deal of broken pottery, such as dishes and cups and saucers, where the house had stood. Later the Norco Bridge *[now Hamner]* was built and then came the big flood of 1938, which swept away the road. After this the state engineers raised the road about four or five feet from the north bank to the bridge. They took their material from the top of the bluff, where the first house of Bandini had stood, taking it all away and then some, so that the treasure of Juan Murietta may be buried in the grade—who knows?

Later Residents Near Bandini Old Adobe Site

Settlers had come into the Guapa about the time of the Civil War. One family named Bittle came about 1860 or so, living below the Bandini house, north of *[present-day]* Norco on the river flats, in their big wagons. The father of the family died and was buried there, and then, in the spring the family moved on.

During the *[Civil]* war a number of the deserters from the Army camped out along the river. One of them lived to be an old man and was well known in Corona. He was the first American to live on the Guapa, but other settlers soon moved in. They would live for a few days or weeks in the old abandoned Bandini house, or leave their supplies there while they were building their own homes. Most of their houses were good frame buildings.

By 1867 they had started a school in a house owned by Mr. Sam Pine; its first teacher was T.J. Ellis, its second H.C. Brooks. The school district was first called Juappa, spelled with two p's. The next year the name was changed to Juapa. The district lapsed in 1879 *[the same year the title to Jurupa-Stearns was confirmed]*, at which time the schoolhouse was on the river flat one half mile west of Adams Avenue *[Hamner]* just below the Bandini house.

Most of the people lived on the north side of the river. Remaining high after a storm, it could not be crossed for days, and children who lived on the south side of the river often stayed with families on the north side until the river subsided.

The Pine family, coming to the river in 1861 and living in the old Bandini house while they were building for themselves, lived on the Guapa for two or three years; then they moved to some government land on the west line of Rincon.

On the south side were Jacob and Joshua Casteel and one of their sisters who had married John St. Marrie, a Frenchman from Quebec.

Margaret Walkinshaw, now Mrs. McCarty, lived in the old Bandini house for a short time and tells, as Arcadia did, of the difficulty of carrying water up the cliff to do the household work. But also there were good times to remember—picnics, dances, and religious gatherings.

As the Casteel and St. Marrie families broke up and left the Ranch, the Guapa began to look the same as it had when Arcadia and her Indian servants had passed over it fifty years before. Only the broken walls remained of the Bandini house. However, a great change was on the way. Men were wondering if there was not some way to get water on the dry plains of Jurupa Rancho. There was, but it took a long time—thirty years or more, with many failures.

Milton Vale put down a well and built a house, only to find that he was just inside of the Grant line, so he lost his claim. The place, known for years as the Vale Ranch, is now the Imbach Ranch *[west of Archibald at Cloverdale/Limonite—may have influenced adoption of the school district name East Vale]*.

A new plan was thought of. It was to gather the river water below the narrows—where underground water was forced to the surface through the valley's contraction—into a large canal five or six miles long high up on the northern slope. This would place a large part of the western end of Jurupa under irrigation.

The land to be irrigated was located to the east, north, and west of the Fuller Ranch and was called the Kingston Tract. The Fuller brothers were at that time there, but they had very small holdings and were not interested in the Kingston Tract. *[Other sources imply that Fuller Ranch originally (circa 1891) included land south of present-day Schleisman between Sumner and Hamner that came to be included in Kingston tract before 1915.]* Their place was known as the Fuller Ranch or Pioneer Trucking Company, for they had located their horses and mules on the good pasture of the river bottom. Their brother-in-law, Fred Zucker, had a store in Old Cucamonga, and the post office at South Cucamonga was called Zucker until it was changed to Guasti.

The ditch, started in 1891, was a costly affair. There were a number of arroyos to cross, some four or five hundred feet wide and quite deep, needing a trestle fifteen to eighteen feet high.

A number of streets were graded at this time: Adams *[Hamner]*, Cleveland *[Scholar Way]*, Harrison, Citrus, and others. A number of parcels of land were also contracted for.

Mr. Woods and his two sons came in 1891, setting out 125 acres of prunes—prunes were bringing $75 a ton at that time. Promised 1,000 inches of water for the 700 acres they had contracted for; for a time they had plenty of water, but, when the trees were about two years old, the water was turned off. A severe north wind blew the flume down. It was not rebuilt. The company, having spent all it could afford to, made no effort to keep up the ditch, so there was no water for the settlers. For several years the Woods family struggled to keep the trees alive by hauling water, but were at last forced to give up and move away. Their neighbors had already done so, for, due to three dry years, they had not been able to even get their seed back.

At this time there was great excitement over the Cana Agrio (sour cane) plant, which grew in the sand hills on the Cucamonga plains. It was thought to be good for making a fluid for tanning leather. Gangs of men dug up the roots and hauled them to what is now Fontana. They cut off the eye for planting, and then cut, dried, and sacked the roots and shipped them out of the country. A large sum of money was spent before it was found out that the project would not pay. However, it had enabled the settlers to earn a little money.

The people of the district carried on dry grain farming for a number of years, but, about 1904, they began to drill wells. Finding that there was plenty of water underground, they put in pumps. The first pumps were very cumbersome, but later the new turbines were used. They literally poured the water out of the ground, and soon there were many prosperous ranches in the Eastvale, Mountain View, Union Joint, and Glen Avon districts. Among the early settlers who had pumps were Oscar Ford, Martin Van Wig, and W.F. Eldridge.

The Eastvale School District was formed in 1893 to take in all of the Kingston Tract and the old *[school]* district of Juapa, which had lapsed in 1879. The trustees were O.B. Fuller and Dave Yount. Among the pupils were the Grotzinger children. The mother was Julia Casteel, who had gone to school in the early Juapa and *[La]* Sierra districts and had been forced to leave, when the Grant was turned over to the Stearns Rancho *[1879—the year she turned twelve]*. She had now come back and lived in the Eastvale section for the next fifty years. *[Julia Grotzinger, born in 1867, is listed in public records including U.S. Census 1940 at Temescal Township. She died in 1951.]*

Appendix B

HISTORY TIMELINE FOR INLAND EMPIRE

Years before 1938, events at Ontario and east, from *San Bernardino Sun,* 30 October 2007

1826—*November 26*—Jedediah Strong Smith and his party arrives at San Gabriel Mission via the Inland Valley, completing the first overland trek from the then–United States to Southern California.

1839—Tiburcio Tapia was awarded Rancho Cucamonga by Governor Juan Alvarado.

1842—*November 9*—Arguably the first community in the Inland Valley, Agua Mansa, was founded by Mexicans from Abiquiu in northern New Mexico on the banks of the Santa Ana River in southern Rialto. The party came overland on the Spanish Trail and set up a farming community. Most of it was washed away in the floods of 1862. Its cemetery, founded in 1852, remains on a rise along Agua Mansa Road and is now a county museum.

1846—*September 26–27*—At Isaac Williams' Chino ranch, a group of Americans fought the only local battle of the Mexican War. They eventually surrendered to Mexican forces, but since most of them were married to Mexican women, most were released soon after.

1848—Tiburcio Tapia, owner of Rancho Cucamonga, dies, and his heirs sell the rancho, which included his adobe atop Red Hill. Rumors persist even today that he buried his fortune somewhere near his adobe, but it has never been found.

1850—Raimundo Yorba built the California ranch adobe [later] known as the Yorba-Slaughter Adobe on a hill above Chino Creek through 1853. It served as a Butterfield Stage stop from 1859–1863. It was sold to Fenton M. Slaughter in 1868.

1851—*June*—A column of wagons with Mormons from Utah comes out of Cajon Pass. The settlers would ultimately found the city of San Bernardino after buying land from the Lugos.

1853—*April 26*—San Bernardino County was formed. It included what is today most of Riverside County. First meeting of the Board of Supervisors was not until May 19, 1855.

1854—*Oct. 13*—Isaac Slover, a mountain man who settled in western Colton, was killed by a bear he was trying to kill in Cajon Pass. A mountain along Interstate 10 being torn down for limestone and a Fontana street is named for him.

1856—*July 4*—Competing Independence Day celebrations went on in San Bernardino. One was a traditional event put on by Louis Rubidoux and his supporters, the other was the Mormon celebration with many anti-federal government themes, a reflection of the threats against the Mormon home of Utah by the federal government.

1862—*January 22*—A flood struck that was probably the greatest in the Inland Valley in recorded history. In the East Fork of the San Gabriel River just west of today's Mt. Baldy Village, the flood wiped out the thriving gold camp of Eldoradoville. Flood control experts estimate the Santa Ana River was carrying 100,000 cubic feet of water per second at its height. The Missouri River by contrast carries 76,000 cubic feet on average. The first real community in the Inland Valley, Agua Mansa, was wiped out by the flood.

November 17—John Rains was murdered near Mud Springs (San Dimas). He owned Rancho Cucamonga. He was married to Maria Merced Williams, daughter of the former owner of Rancho Santa Ana del Chino, Isaac Williams. Rains' killers were never found though his radical pro-Southern friends believed his wife was somehow to blame.

1864—Nicholas Earp brought his family from Iowa to Redlands. Sons Wyatt, Virgil, and Morgan later went east to become lawmen. Virgil would later become the first marshal of Colton.

1871—*May 9*—Debt-ridden Rancho Cucamonga was foreclosed on by Isaias Hellman.

1874—*July 3*—Isaias Hellman forms the Cucamonga Homestead Association to sell land north of Base Line Road and west of Hermosa in Alta Loma.

Also in 1874—Former ship captain Joseph S. Garcia built a house northeast of Highland and Etiwanda avenues in Etiwanda.

1881—*Thanksgiving Day*—Joseph S. Garcia sells his Etiwanda ranch to the Chaffey brothers, their first acquisition in the Inland Valley.

Also in 1881—Richard Gird, using money he got for selling his successful gold claim in Tombstone Arizona, buys Rancho de Chino and set out to lay out the future city of Chino.

1882—*November 23*—George Chaffey and his brother William formed their land company and began selling land in what would become Ontario.

December—George Chaffey, at his Etiwanda ranch, ignited the first electric light in the Inland Valley, and in fact all of California. It was the first electric light powered by hydroelectric power west of the Rockies.

December 11—Grading began on the wide Euclid Avenue in Ontario.

Also in 1882—Chaffey installed the first telephone line in the Inland Valley, extending from Etiwanda to San Bernardino.

1883—*March 17*—Cornerstone laid for the new Chaffey College of Agriculture in Ontario.

1887—*February 17*—The Semi-Tropic Land and Water Company was founded and bought 28,500 acres of land west of Lytle Creek in today's Rialto for the purpose of the development.

April 7—First sale of lots in Claremont.

May—The first sale of land of the boomtown of Magnolia was held in what would become Upland. Sales were bad and one year later, the project was foreclosed.

May—Arrival of the first trains [Santa Fe Railroad, two routes, via Upland and via Santa Ana Canyon] through the Inland Valley from the east. Development boomed: by fall there were 25 "cities" between Los Angeles and San Bernardino.

June—Lots were being sold in Marquette, a soon-to-fail community in what is now north Ontario just off Baker Avenue and south of today's Metrolink tracks.

October—Two small communities—Hermosa and the Iowa Tract—merge in Alta Loma to create the name Ioamosa, though it gradually disappeared in favor of Alta Loma.

December 13—A strong Santa Ana wind blew down the Cucamonga Methodist Church at Base Line and Archibald.

1891—*April 17*—Ceremony marks the founding of the community Rochester, a short-lived development along Rochester Avenue south of Arrow Route in Rancho Cucamonga. The place failed for lack of water source.

December 10—Ontario was incorporated as a city. Residents voted 40-31 in favor of incorporation on November 21.

1893—*August 14*—Riverside County formally created out of land previously in San Bernardino and San Diego counties.

December 11—Chaffey College of Agriculture defeated University of Southern California, 32–6, in a football game played in Ontario.

1895—*January 4*—Robbers hold up the Ontario State Bank on Euclid Avenue and steal $4,875. Channing B. Barnes was later caught and tried for the theft. An audience of young women watched the proceedings of the trial involving the handsome, dashing Barnes. He was sentenced to a relatively light sentence of six years at San Quentin.

Also in 1895—Earl H. Richardson came to Ontario and began working for Charles Frankish's electrical plant. He later invented the first practical household iron and created the brand name, "Hotpoint." He later sold his firm to General Electric which made the irons in Ontario for many years.

1899—*December 25*—An estimated 6.6 earthquake struck in Riverside causing little damage in the Inland Valley.

1903—*January 3*—Former slave and famed educator Booker T. Washington spoke to a packed house at the Methodist Church in Ontario. Later he addressed an audience at Pomona College in Claremont.

1905—*Ontario Republican* founded as a weekly newspaper.

1906—*May 5*—Upland residents vote, 182-19, to incorporate as a city, which became official on May 15.

1907—*October 10*—The Ontario town council fired Marshal Edward McMannis because he failed to fill out his official oath bond, which office holders were required to complete. Actually, the council wanted to get rid of McMannis, which had annoyed many in the community, and found a loophole to kick him out of office.

1908—*May 30*—The Women's Relief Corps dedicated a monument to Union Civil War veterans at Bellevue Cemetery in Ontario. The base of the monument is still there, but the copper statue is in storage after being vandalized many times. The WRC was a women's organization supporting the Grand Army of the Republic, an American Legion–type organization of Union war veterans.

July 4—A drinking fountain on Euclid Avenue in Ontario was dedicated by the local chapter of the Woman's Christian Temperance Union. It has moved several times and is now in the central median of Euclid in downtown.

August 15—Perhaps the first "flight" in the Inland Valley was by Harry F. Wright, who rode a balloon, pushed by hot air from a bonfire on the ground in Ontario. He went up about 3,000 feet and then jumped out with a parachute. It was as part of a promotion for Ontario merchants.

November 15—A two-balloon transcontinental race began from Los Angeles, with the goal of reaching New York. One balloon went 15 miles, the wrong way, while the second, the "American," reached Ontario, and then tied up for the night. The "race" ended the second day when it could go no farther than Corona.

December—Ontario was visited by Leon Livingston, then the most famous tramp in America. He was known as A-No. 1 and wrote numerous books about his adventures. He spent some time traveling with famed author Jack London.

1910—*February 28*—Chino formally becomes an incorporated city.

September 12—*Ontario Republican* became a daily.

1911—*January 7*—Many of the orchard trees in the area were destroyed due to well-below-freezing temperatures. Farmers burned straw or hay in a futile attempt to warm the air around their trees.

January 11—Didier Masson flies copies of a Los Angeles newspaper to San Bernardino despite crashing once in Cucamonga. He was supposed to stop in Pomona on the way out but got lost. He was on his way back to Pomona to perform in front of a large group when he crashed again.

October 11—California women won the right to vote in a special election which also added the recall, referendum, and initiative to the state Constitution. All Inland Valley cities and communities voted to give women the vote except for Spadra (west Pomona) and Cucamonga.

October 31—Rialto voters approved incorporation of the city by a 135-72 margin. It became official on November 17.

Also in 1911—Pomona votes "dry," banning alcohol sales nine years before Prohibition. Legal sales would not return to the city until 1933 at Prohibition's end.

Also in 1911—Crombie and H.L. Allen buy the *Ontario Republican.*

1912—*January 1*—The *Republican* becomes the *Daily Report.*

April 11—At a meeting of residents of Ioamosa area of Alta Loma met, a committee was selected to raise money to encourage the Pacific Electric rail line to alter its rail route to run north through Alta Loma and Etiwanda.

1914—*April 13*—Pool halls could remain open in Ontario. A ballot measure to bar such establishments was defeated, 622-612.

July 11—The Pacific Electric trolley line was completed from Claremont to San Bernardino. Through the efforts of Russian immigrant Peter Demens, Alta Loma interests raised enough money to have the line bend north across today's Rancho Cucamonga providing rail access for farmers there. The rails have been pulled up along the route but plans are under way for a series of walking trails throughout the area.

1915—*November 14*—The Liberty Bell, being hauled to the world's fair in San Francisco, made brief appearances in Ontario and Pomona. Throngs turned out to see the bell during the five-minute stops in each town. It was the only time the bell has been moved west of Chicago.

1916—*January*—Flooding destroyed several homes along Cucamonga Creek on the Upland–Alta Loma border. A fight was only narrowly averted after Alta Loma residents thought Upland had blocked the creek's flow pushing it east of Red Hill, flooding their area. Mother Nature had actually done the blocking.

July 28—Perhaps the first aircraft fatality in the Inland Valley occurred in a freak accident in Alta Loma. Residents watched a military flyer, who landed the day before because of engine trouble, take off. The plane stalled upon take off and slammed into a car killing a mother and her 4-year-old boy.

Also in 1916—Chaffey College becomes a publicly supported junior college in Ontario. It claims to be the oldest community college in California.

1918—During the great so-called Spanish influenza epidemic, more Americans died from the flu in 1918 and 1919 than all the combat deaths of the 20th century, about 500,000. First Ontario city death came October 21: Joseph Morgon, a 28-year-old telephone employee.

1919—*May 7*—Led by Police Chief Jedd Sawyer, Upland police captured five criminals. Their crime was playing poker in the second story of the Colborn building.

1920—*November*—Ontario residents vote, 1,093-729, to bar motion pictures on Sundays. Vote came after a city-wide uproar over showing movies on the Sabbath.

1924—*March 1*—San Bernardino County was poised to hire controversial "Rainmaker" Charles M. Hatfield to break the drought that plagued the Inland Valley. Just before he could be hired, the belated winter rains arrived.

June 21—The first trip of an airline out of what is today's Ontario airport was flown by Waldo Waterman from Ontario to Big Bear Lake. On the return trip, he crashed into the lake, killing one passenger and injuring Ontario Mayor W.D. Ball.

September 8—A massive parade and cross burning at Chaffey High School by the Ontario Order of the Knights of the Ku Klux Klan was held in which 150 new members were initiated.

1926—*November 11*—Route 66 (and other federal highways) came into existence by the federal government. The number was originally supposed to be 60, but a Kentucky governor demanded that for a highway in its state. As a compromise, the Chicago–Los Angeles road became the distinctive 66.

November—The brand name "Sunkist" was first introduced by the California Fruit Growers Exchange, which grew out of Co-ops in the Inland Valley.

1928—*March*—The U.S. Rabbit Experiment Station was opened in Fontana to research breeding and raising of rabbits for food. It operated until 1962.

October 6—The Euclid Avenue trolley line was closed between the mountains and Ontario. It was originally powered by mules (which rode at the back of the trolleys on the way down). Closure of the line also allowed placement of Madonna of the Trail statue to be built in the rail bed.

1929—*February*—Canadian Gordon S. Northcott was convicted for killing numerous young boys at his ranch in Wineville (today's Mira Loma). His mother Louise was convicted as an accessory and spent several years at San Quentin where she was on October 2 1930, when her son was hanged nearby.

February 1—The Madonna of the Trail statue dedicated at Euclid and Foothill in Upland by the Daughters of the American Revolution.

August 18—The first women's cross-country air race flew over the Inland Valley from Santa Monica, ending its first day in San Bernardino. More than 5,000 people lined the landing strip in San Bernardino to greet the 18 fliers.

October 29—Stock market crash. On that day, Ontario banker Oscar Arnold gave a talk and said that the crash of the stock market was good for this area as it would free up more money for real estate.

November 25—Frank Baumgarteker, a wealthy Los Angeles businessman and Cucamonga vineyard owner, disappeared without a trace in Los Angeles. Rumors said he was killed because he refused a demand from Chicago mobsters to sell them his vineyard.

December 22—The state dedicated a state game farm in the Los Serranos area of what is now Chino Hills. It would raise turkeys, pheasants, quail, partridge, and chukar to be "planted" in Southern California areas for hunters.

December 29—Ontario buys 30 acres for an airport east of town on what would became Ontario International Airport.

1930—*October 11*—R.W. Agnew faced a 6-month sentence for stealing walnuts in Ontario. He told a deputy he actually wouldn't mind being jailed where it's warm and the food is free. The deputy told Judge Jim

Sharp, who gave him a suspended 30-day sentence and kicked him out of town.

November 1—The community of Wineville officially changed its name to Mira Loma. The change was made to create a "drier" name in those Prohibition days.

1933—*March 10*—The Inland Valley was rocked by the Long Beach earthquake. Damage locally was minimal but the area sent many truckloads of relief goods to assist the victims along the coast.

December 5 – Prohibition ends with the 21st Amendment. The Cucamonga Valley Wine Company celebrates by sending President Franklin Roosevelt a case of Inland Valley wine.

1935—*February*—Harold Vermilyea of Ontario was found guilty of murder in Ontario, Canada. He used an elaborate scheme to pretend to take a motor trip when instead he took 2 planes and a train to return to his hometown and murder his mother. An alert Ontario detective found the clues that resulted in his hanging. The case received national attention because transcontinental plane rides, especially for criminal intent, were still rare.

August—Jedd Sawyer, Upland's only police chief, dies at 57 after 29 years of service. He was remarkable because he had only one arm.

1937—*January*—The area was hit with three weeks of sub-freezing cold that damaged trees and resulted in heavy smudging, in which oil was ignited in hopes the smoke would hold in the heat and keep the tree safe from frost. In one night alone, 770,000 gallons of oil was burned in Southern California.

1938—*Early March*—Tremendous flooding left the Inland Valley and Orange County (where the Santa Ana River flows out) under water. It was the largest flood of the 20th century and possibly only surpassed in recorded history by the floods of 1862. About 32 inches of rain fell March 1 and 2 at Kelly's Camp near Cucamonga Peak. Camp Baldy (where Mt. Baldy Village is today) was destroyed.

BIBLIOGRAPHY

Books and Formal Reports

Asay, Jeff. *Union Pacific in the Los Angeles Basin.* Berkeley, CA: Signature Press, 2010.

Brown, John, Jr., and James Boyd. *History of San Bernardino and Riverside Counties.* Chicago: Lewis Publishing Company, 1922.

Bynon, A.A., and Son. *History and Directory of Riverside County, 1893–4 (originally volume 1).* Riverside, CA: Historical Commission Press, 1992.

Cleland, Robert Glass. *The Cattle on a Thousand Hills, Southern California 1850–1880 (second edition).* San Marino, CA: Huntington Library, 1951.

Eldridge, Fred, and Stanley Reynolds. *Corona California Commentaries.* Corona, CA: Heritage Committee of the Friends of the Corona Public Library, 1986.

Engelhardt, Father Zephyrin, O.F.M. *San Gabriel Mission and the Beginnings of Los Angeles.* San Gabriel, CA: Mission San Gabriel, 1927.

Garner, Walter T. "Arcadia and the Forgotten Guapa." Jurupa Valley, CA: Jurupa Mountains Discovery Center, 1967 (reprint 1981).

Greenwood, Roberta S., and John S. Foster. *Context and Evaluation of Historical Sites in the Prado Basin.* Los Angeles: U.S. Army Corps of Engineers, 1990.

Gunther, Jane Davies. *Riverside County, California, Place Names—Their Origins and Their Stories.* Riverside, CA: Gunther, 1984.

Hart, John Mason. *Empire and Revolution. The Americans in Mexico since the Civil War.* Berkeley: University of California Press, 2002.

Johnson, Ann H., and Susan D. Buchel. *The Century of El Rincón—Historical Synthesis of the Bandini-Cota Adobe, Prado Flood Control Basin, Riverside County, California.* Los Angeles: Department of the Army, Corps of Engineers, June 1983.

Kennedy, David M., Lizabeth Cohen and Thomas A Bailey. *The American Pageant (13th Edition)*. Boston: Houghton Mifflin, 2006.
Langenwalter, Paul E., II, and James Brock. *Phase II Archaeological Studies Prado Basin and the Lower Santa Ana River*. Los Angeles: U.S. Army Corps of Engineers, 1985.
Lech, Steve. *Along the Old Roads: A History of the Portion of Southern California that Became Riverside County, 1772–1893*. Riverside, CA: self-published, 2004.
Lewis Publishing Company. *Illustrated History of Southern California*. Chicago: Lewis Publishing Company, 1890.
Lyman, Edward Leo. *San Bernardino: The Rise and Fall of a California Community*. Salt Lake City, UT: Signature Books, 1996.
Mitchell, Patrick. *Santa Ana River Guide*. Berkeley: Wilderness Press, 2006.
Monroy, Douglas. *Thrown Among Strangers*. Berkeley: University of California Press, 1990.
Patterson, Tom. *Landmarks of Riverside.* Riverside, CA: Press-Enterprise Company, 1964.
Peterson, Charles S., and Alfred Cumming. *Utah History Encyclopedia.* Salt Lake City: University of Utah Press, 1994
Puntney, William David. *Jurupa: Never So Far Was Arcadia.* In John R. Brumgardt, *Historical Portraits of Riverside County*. Riverside, CA: Riverside County Historical Commission, 1977.
Rensch, H.E., and E.G. Rensch. *Historic Spots in California: The Southern Counties (1932 edition)*. Stanford, CA: Stanford University Press, 1932.
Shockey, Ralph N., and Marie F. *Shockey History and Genealogy, Vol. II.* Frederick, MD: William Terry Browne, 1981.
Signor, John R. *The Los Angeles and Salt Lake Railroad Company: Union Pacific's Historic Salt Lake Route.* San Marino, CA: Golden West Books, 1988.
Van Dyke, T.S. *Millionaires of a Day.* New York: Fords, Howard & Hulbert, 1890. (Reprint available via Amazon.)
Wright, Doris Marion. *A Yankee in Mexican California: Abel Stearns, 1798–1848.* Santa Barbara, CA: Wallace Hebberd, 1977.

E-MAIL RESOURCES

Hollister, William. 2011.
Rozzi, Ted E. 24 October 2001.

JOURNALS AND OTHER PERIODICALS

Baker, Patricia. "The Bandini Family." *Journal of San Diego History* 15, no. 1 (1969).

Beattie, George William. "Development of Travel between Southern Arizona and Los Angeles as It Related to the San Bernardino Valley." *Annual Publication of the Historical Society of Southern California* 13, no. 2 (1925). Reprint: University of California Press.

Bowman, J.N. "Driving the Last Spike at Promontory, 1869." *California Historical Society Quarterly* XXXVI, no. 2 (June 1957) and XXXVI, no. 3 (September 1957). cprr.org/Museum/Bowman_Last_Spike_CHS.html.

Iversen, Eve. "Wine at the California Missions." 1998 California Mission Studies Association Annual Conference, San Juan Capistrano.

Patterson, Tom. "Rancho Boundaries." *Riverside Historical Society Journal* 14 (2000).

"Personal Notes." *Bus Transportation* 1 (June 1922): 363.

Warner, J.J. "Reminiscences of Early California from 1831–1846." *Historical Society of Southern California, Annual Publications* 1907–1908.

NEWSPAPERS

Corona Daily Independent

Los Angeles Times

Riverside Press and Enterprise

WEBSITES

"California in the Civil War." wikipedia.org/wiki/California_in_the_American_Civil_War.

Cowgill, Jacob. prairieheritagefarm.com/2009_04_01_archive.html.

ERHA. erha.org/motortransitstage/mts.htm.

Hoffman, Abraham. "Movers and Shakers Who Moved and Shook L.A.: The Diversity of Our City's Nineteenth Century Heritage." socalhistory.org/articles/movers-and-shakers-who-moved-and-shook-l-a-the-diversity-of-our-citys-19th-century-heritage.html.

Malakoff.com/marshall.htm.

Patterson, Tom. "Triumph and Tragedy of Dalip Saund." *California Historian*, June 1992. www.pbs.org/rootsinthesand/dalip.pdf.

Pourade, R.F. *History of San Diego*. Sandiegohistory.org/books/pourade/index.htm.

RCFlood. "Riverside County Flood Control and Water Conservation District; First 50 Years; Pre-District Years." rcflood.org/RCFCInternetText/History.html.

Regional Trails. santaanarivertrail.org/home.html.

University of California–Davis. "Viticulture." iv.ucdavis.edu/Viticultural_Information.

Wilkman, Jon. Socalhistory.org/biographies/arcadia-bandini-stearns-debaker.html.

ABOUT THE AUTHORS

Both authors of this brief history grew up in northwestern Riverside County, near the Santa Ana River and present-day Eastvale.

Kim Jarrell Johnson is a lifelong resident of present-day Jurupa Valley and an avid participant in civic affairs of the region. She enjoys exploring the background this bustling metropolis to better understand its recent metamorphosis. She has written several books, including *Jurupa* (2005) and *Rubidoux, California* (2007) in the Arcadia Images of America series and *Wicked Jurupa Valley* (2012) in The History Press Wicked series, that examine the diverse culture of this corner of Riverside County.

Loren Meissner grew up in Riverdale Acres. This tract is a mile or two distant, east of Wineville Avenue and south of Limonite (see Chapter 4), but it has always been in the same elementary and secondary school districts as central Eastvale. Loren attended Eastvale Elementary School on Sumner Avenue between 1934 and 1941, graduated from Corona High School in 1945 and later moved to northern California. When he read in some present-day blogs that the history of Eastvale began when dairies moved eastward from Los Angeles County about 1970, Loren's skeptical reaction to such assertions led him to this project.